YOGA FOR PELVIC FLOOR HEALTH:

A Whole-Body Approach to Strengthening & Healing

Leah Wrobel

Editor: Lisa Kremer

Design: Dorit Talpaz

Photography: Alicia Osborn

Portrait photo: Ieva Vi

This book is not intended as a substitute for medical advice. Readers should consult their physicians if there is any doubt regarding the effects of any exercise in this book on their health.

ISBN: 978-87-973568-0-7

www.leahwrobel.com

Link to free audio playlist of all practices

https://soundcloud.com/user-602591914-277886242/sets/practice

Introduction 5

Some Anatomy 17

How Do We Talk About Pelvic Floor Training? 25

Isuf – A Rich and Vital Way to Engage the Pelvic Floor 31

- Non-harming in the Face of Painful Truth: The Attitude of *Ahimsa & Satya* 32
- Cultivating *Isuf* with Six Techniques for Training the Pelvic Floor 35
- *Isuf* in Action: Fundamental Exercises for Training the Pelvic Floor 54

Nurturing Pelvic Health: Yoga Practices & Personal Stories 69

Spiraling, Flowing Energy of *Bandhas* 157

An Organic Part of Our Wonderful Self 165

Sample Practice Flows 166

Acknowledgments 169

Endnotes 172

Bibliography 174

INTRODUCTION

I have been working with my body from a very young age, dancing since childhood, and practicing and teaching yoga for more than two decades. Yet for most of my life, my pelvic floor was a weak link for me, and even a bit of a mystery. I had a healthy sex life and gave birth naturally twice, but still, both in yoga practice and in daily life, the base of my pelvis felt under-active or over-emphasized–either way, not organic–and definitely not like it was meant to be: strong, powerful, and in sync with the rest of my body.

As a child, I remember leaking urine if I laughed too hard. When I had my first baby, and more so with my second, leaking would occur with jumping, running, sneezing, and coughing. Stress incontinence–lack of control when abdominal pressure is suddenly increased–is considered "normal," especially among women after giving birth. And most pharmacies in the United States, it seems, offer ever-growing aisles packed with pads, special panties for women, and adult diapers. When I sought help, the professional and medical advice I received caused me extreme frustration. Midwives in California advised me to do up to 250 Kegels a day: *"Do them when you chop your salad." "Do them at every stop light when you drive."* A urologist in Florida did not skip a beat before recommending surgery to insert a mesh sling under the bladder, and an esteemed gynecologist seemed puzzled by my issues and wondered aloud if perhaps something in the angle of my urethra was causing the leakage. People around me disregarded my concerns because I seemed strong and stable in my yoga practice. I finally understood that looking outside myself for a solution was a waste of time, and could even be harmful. I just wanted to sneeze or run around with my kids without needing to change my pants.

I have moved around a lot in my life—born and raised in Israel to a Danish mother and American father, later living in the US, and for a two-year spell in France between the births of my US-born children, one born on the east coast and the other on the west. These many cultures and perspectives have shaped my outlook on life, health, and the body. In France I had the opportunity to learn some French secrets for what seemed like a more balanced life. I was exposed to the uninhibited pleasure of enjoying good food and wine; I walked to work and walked my daughter to school; and I learned about complementary medicine, as my primary care doctor was also a homeopathic doctor. I also learned that every woman in France enjoys access to pelvic floor physical therapy six weeks after delivery as part of her routine health care. There it is taken for granted that female health is important, that a healthy sex life is important, and that talking about it is not a big deal.

When I moved back to the US, I carried that message with me. My curiosity and willingness to speak openly about pelvic floor health yielded fascinating conversations; mountains of emotions; many, many questions; loads of contradictory material; and a surprisingly large number of folks resigned to living with pelvic floor disorders, suffering in silence yet wishing to talk. Some were so dissatisfied with the solutions they had been offered that they just gave up seeking, and others were so burdened by shame that they had never sought a solution at all.

I changed my approach toward my own health and began looking, not for one-stop solutions, but for *inspiration*—from books, anatomy lessons, Feldenkrais teachers, Pilates teachers, dancers, physical therapists, and most of all from my personal yoga practice. All of this information was processed through my "yoga eye" of mindful attention, leading me on a journey that circled back to close the gap between how I related to my body in yoga and how I related to my pelvic floor. What was once a weak link transformed into a vibrant area interconnected with and integral to my whole body. And so, I was inspired. I wanted to teach pelvic floor health and I wanted to do it right.

सत्य

I knew that I had to offer an integrative class, subtle and layered, different from what is most widely prescribed as the be-all and end-all—Kegels. Seeking professional support, I reached out to Lisa Whiting, a local physical therapist specializing in pelvic health. Having lived in Israel and Europe, where pelvic specialists are more common, it astonished me that in the capital of Florida where I was living at the time, there was only one person in this field! What surprised me most about our initial conversation was her enthusiasm about being able to refer those whom she called her "pain patients" to a suitable yoga class.

Until then I had thought about pelvic floor issues mainly in terms of lack of control or weakness. This was, of course, aligned with my personal experience. Yet it is simplistic. I was aware of the staggering numbers, with studies showing that over fifty percent of all women experience urinary incontinence at some point in their lives. But I was unaware that 33% of women report a history of chronic pelvic pain,[1] and that so many suffer from overly tight pelvic floor muscles. A young student helped me understand this new territory that I had entered when she explained, "My vagina hurts ALL THE TIME."

सत्य

Tell a person who has overly tight pelvic floor muscles that other people have their inner organs collapsing through the lower openings and see the horror on their face if they have never before heard about prolapse. Tell a person with prolapse or incontinence that other women cannot use a tampon or wear jeans because of the level of pain they experience and see the relief on their face that this isn't what they are personally dealing with. When we talk about the pelvic floor, emotions are provoked, and when we add any sense that things aren't functioning as they should be, emotions surge.

Katelyn's eyes well up when she tells me about her prolapse. She describes how she saw and touched the bulging of her inner organs through her vaginal opening, and how she felt her body had let her down, leading to anger, depression, and anxiety. Another student, Clara, whose past trauma has left her feeling that this whole area should remain untouched, tells me "This is a part of my body that has been ignored for so many years . . . *and it has all that sadness."* For men it is no less "shameful" when having an erection is challenging or when suffering incontinence and leakage. A few of the men I work with talk about pelvic floor problems that accompany prostate cancer recovery or are the result of an accident.

While people would have no problem mentioning to their yoga teacher (or friends and family) that they have a twisted ankle or injured shoulder, it is rare to hear complaints about chronic constipation or urge incontinence. A knee injury can leave us feeling aggravated, impatient, and sad if we cannot continue doing the activities that we love such as biking, running, or maybe even sitting cross-legged for meditation. But pelvic floor disorders are different because of how *private* this information feels, and the way it impacts the most mundane and intimate aspects of our life. Stained pants, inability to enjoy intercourse, difficulty sitting or going to the bathroom, all have a huge impact on one's relationships, activities, and self-esteem.

Just as the pelvic floor can hold sadness and shame, it can also hold trauma. It is my experience that many more people than I would like to think carry within them experiences of sexual trauma, ranging from the extreme form of rape or child abuse, to more familiar forms such as repeated objectification and unwanted touching. These experiences oftentimes lead to detachment of mind from body, specifically the pelvic floor.

Fear is another strong emotion associated with pelvic floor disorders—fear of lack of control, exposure, or of being humiliated. Sadly, healthcare professionals can contribute to these negative emotions and scars. I have heard too many stories about dismissiveness to outright shaming and ridicule. This is not to say that there aren't many wonderful, supportive doctors and nurses out there—*of course there are!* Perhaps what is most lacking in our system is a general belief in our capacity to gain control and play an active role in our own healing process.

सत्य

When we connect to the base of the pelvis, regain sensation, and find a flow of energy, relief washes over us. The vitality we feel is visible. And though it is so incredibly obvious that the pelvic floor is integral to a functioning body, it is equally incredible to meet so many people who have no such idea. Feeling sensation, even just at the beginning of the healing process, empowers us with a sense of trust in our bodies that can evolve into wonder. Even though I have continuously worked on my body for years, when an abrupt sneeze comes, or if I can do some jumping jacks in my living room with my son without any leakage, I feel good, strong, and proud.

Another dimension of healing and building strength is a positive sexual outlook. When I asked students to share their stories for this book, practically no one wrote about sex. I attribute this to American cultural attitudes regarding sex being either over-the-top or off-limits. Yet between classes, or as a joke or a whisper at the end of a workshop, I learn about happy intercourse with increasingly happy partners; longer, stronger orgasms; and newfound confidence and pleasure. Feeling pleasure from our bodies through healthy function, movement, and intimacy is, on all levels, wonderful. And fun. It is almost always a blessed "side effect" of this practice.

सत्य

Why yoga? How is yoga different than physical therapy? Many seek the help of doctors, chiropractors, nutritionists, body workers, acupuncturists, and other medical professionals to heal. When we find the right fit, it is fantastic. Physical therapy for the pelvic floor is a must for certain conditions, and it combines the patient's internal work with constant feedback from the provider—both manually and with the use of biofeedback. But according to my experience and the experience of my students, in order to fully heal and maintain pelvic health, we need to become our own healer. This is where yoga shines. With a teacher or text as our guide, we do the internal work on ourselves and learn to identify our habits. We take responsibility for our own health and learn how to maintain it.

What distinguishes yoga from exercise? Yoga requests a particular flavor of attentiveness, active listening, and willingness to meet ourselves and the sometimes overwhelming emotions connected with the pelvic floor, with compassion and honesty. With the correct attitude toward practice, the body can transform into its own safe space. Listening to the body, and being guided by breath, love for, and patience with oneself, allows for little light bulbs to be lit and the strengthening and healing of our most hidden places to transpire.

सत्य

When I began teaching pelvic health-focused classes and workshops it became immediately clear that when we speak about pelvic floor muscles, most people have no mental grasp of what we are talking about. I am asked if the pelvic floor is the uterus, the sacrum, or the genitals. Although in charge of so much of our life function –going to the bathroom, having intercourse, standing upright–it can be a challenge to find the *feeling* of that place. The complex structure of the pelvis houses a lifetime of misalignment, habits, emotions, inhibitions, social constraints, trauma, etc., all of which can prevent our muscles from easily following instructions. If I lift my arm and ask you to do the same, you can easily imitate that movement. But the pelvic floor is oh-so-private and hidden, and can seem difficult or even impossible to access at times. My hope for this book is that it will make this quest for the *feeling* not only possible but pleasant. And that finally when the pelvic floor will feel *real,* it will no longer be the issue you are working with but will simply become a part of you, an organic part of your wonderful self. So that you may carry yourself, see yourself, and feel yourself, as whole.

HOW TO USE THIS BOOK

This book is not a scientific book. Inspired by my own learning process and my love for yoga, this book maps out ways for you to increase your knowledge and awareness, get educated about your body, and locate and access your pelvic floor through internal observation and through connecting to sensation and feeling. The book begins by introducing some basic anatomy and widespread pelvic floor dysfunctions. Next, a compassionate, nonjudgmental, honest attitude is established as the foundation of yoga for pelvic floor work. You'll learn *how* to work with six techniques–relax, breathe, look, imagine, move, and feel, with an emphasis on the crucial role of correct breathing. And the guiding concept of *isuf*–a vital way to engage and integrate the pelvic floor muscles–will be explained. Easy-to-follow exercises will guide you in training your pelvic floor in conjunction with your whole body. This work will require your full attention. At the core of my methodology is this principle:

> **It is more effective to practice five mindful breaths a day, correctly engaging the pelvic floor muscles and releasing them, than to do a full hour of exercises you don't quite understand, or which you are not truly present for–mind and body.**

The techniques, exercises, and yoga postures for training your pelvic floor are woven together with stories of the healing journeys of nineteen of my students. As I hear my students' voices, I also hear those who suffer in silence. Those who do not know that there are alternative ways of finding strength and healing. Perhaps you will recognize yourself, or a friend, in these stories. My intention is for you to find inspiration, practical teaching, embodiment, and hope. Reading the stories, you may feel drawn to every detail, or you may find yourself indifferent, intrigued, or even burdened by their weight. Give yourself permission to go straight to the practices.

Healing is not linear and not everything works for everyone. I invite you to remain curious and investigative, even playful. As you read this book, use your imagination, and allow your emotional world to be a part of your experience. In addition, I am a big believer in taking care of oneself *before* something stops feeling right. So, for those of you who feel quite alright but are interested in gaining more body awareness, increased blood flow, enhancing your yoga practice or sex life, or just staying proactive about your health as you age, this book is for you, too.

अहिंसा

SOME ANATOMY

Where is and What is the Pelvic Floor?

The pelvic floor is an incredibly complicated and fascinating structure. Layers of muscles, ligaments, and connective tissue weave under, over, and around themselves and the bony structure of the pelvis, to provide a hammock-like base that supports our inner organs. For women, the inner organs of the pelvis include the bowel, uterus, and bladder, with three passages–the urethra, vagina, and anus–going through the pelvic floor. For men, the inner organs include the bowel, prostate, and bladder with two passages, the urethra and anus. These passages are kept closed by ring-like muscles called sphincters that allow us control over relieving the bladder and bowel. At the very center of the pelvic floor, we can find the perineum, which is the dense connective tissue located between the anus and vagina in women, and the area between the anus and scrotum in men.

This entire group of muscles, sixteen bands in total,[2] can be thought of like a sling-shaped trampoline of strong tissue that keeps internal organs supported but has the capacity to allow for relaxation. We can visualize the pelvic floor as if hanging stretched from four corners: the two sitting bones (ischial tuberosity), the pubic bone in the front, and the tailbone in the back (coccyx). Within this group of muscles, we can observe three layers: the superficial layer (includes the bands in the shape of a figure eight and the transverse perineal body as seen in Image 1), the frontal urogenital triangle (includes the muscles connected to the genitalia and urethra), and the back fan,[3] the deepest layer, which is made up of the levator ani muscle group and the coccygeus, sometimes referred to as the pelvic diaphragm. It is important to remember that the layers of the pelvic floor are not simply stacked one upon the other, but create a complex structure where all the muscle, ligaments, and connective tissue work seamlessly together. (To learn more about the anatomy of the pelvic floor see Bibliography for recommended reading.)

Although relief for pelvic floor dysfunction does not come from looking at images, many of my students report how helpful it is to see images and get a basic understanding of their structure and function. Look at the images below and try to locate the different bones, muscles, and openings in your own body.

Female pelvic floor (Image 1)

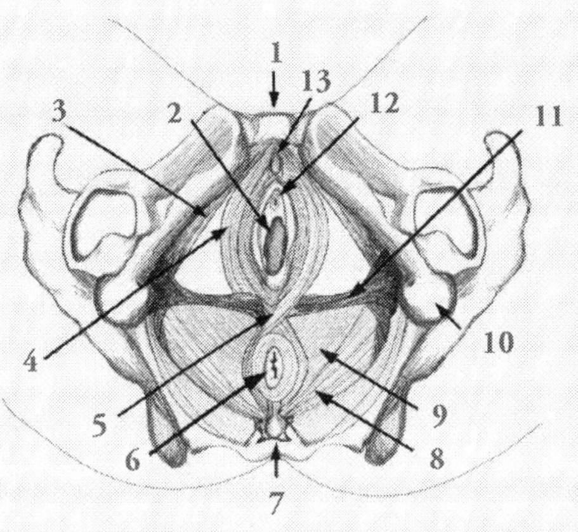

1 Pubic bone
2 Vagina
3 Ischiocavernosus
4 Bulbocavernosus
5 Perineum
6 Anus
7 Coccyx bone
8 Iliococcygeus
9 Pubococcygeus
10 Ischial tuberosity
11 Transverse perineal muscle
12 Urethra
13 Clitoris

Male pelvic floor (Image 2)

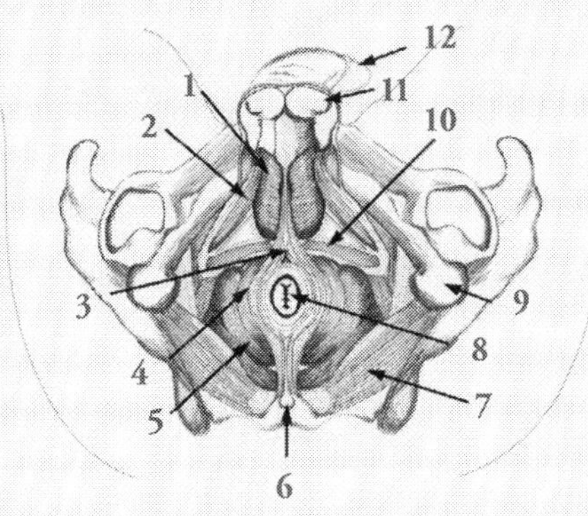

1 Bulbocavernosus
2 Ischiocavernosus
3 Perineal body
4 Levator Ani: Pubococcygeus
5 Iliococcygeus
6 Coccyx bone
7 Gluteus maximus
8 Anus
9 Ischial tuberosity
10 Transversus perineum
11 Testicles
12 Penis

Female anatomy sagittal view (Image 3)

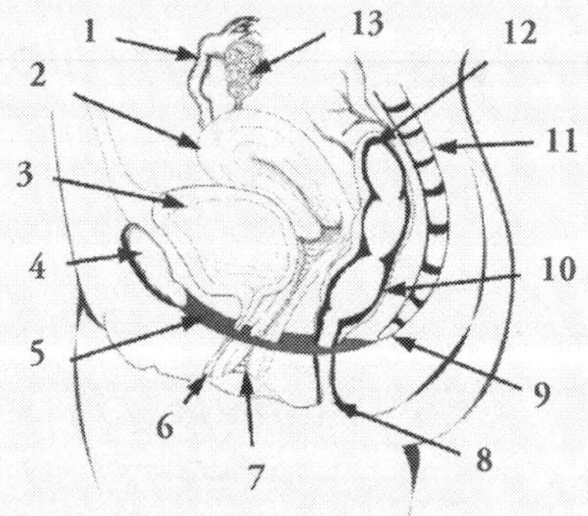

1 Fallopian tube
2 Uterus
3 Bladder
4 Pubic bone
5 Pelvic floor muscles
6 Urethra
7 Vagina
8 Anus
9 Coccyx
10 Rectum
11 Spine
12 Bowel
13 Ovary

Male anatomy sagittal view (Image 4)

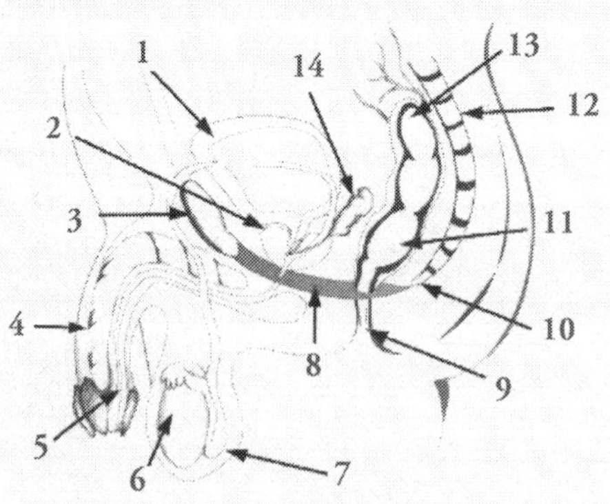

1 Bladder
2 Prostate
3 Pubic Bone
4 Penis
5 Urethra
6 Testicle
7 Scrotum
8 Pelvic floor muscle
9 Anus
10 Coccyx
11 Rectum
12 Spine
13 Bowel
14 Seminal Vesicles

PELVIC FLOOR DYSFUNCTION

The anatomically complex pelvic region can harbor a broad variety of disorders related to structure and function. The origins of pelvic floor dysfunction and their wide-ranging impact can be elusive: musculoskeletal issues can impact bladder, bowel, and sexual function; and vice versa, with dysfunctions causing postural and musculoskeletal issues. This can lead to a vicious cycle of disorders, infections, inflammation, and nerve irritation.[4]

The most common symptomatic pelvic floor dysfunction is urinary incontinence, with 10–58% of women in the US reporting the involuntary loss of urine.[5] This statistic includes both stress and urge incontinence. Stress incontinence occurs when there is pressure on the bladder, such as during coughing, sneezing, and jumping, while urge incontinence presents as a strong urge to urinate with leakage before making it to the bathroom. Another common bladder disorder that is disruptive and painful for both men and women, causing irritation in the bladder lining, is interstitial cystitis. Disorders related to the bowel include diarrhea, constipation, urgency, defecation dysfunction, inflammation of the bowel and rectum, and fecal incontinence.[6] Pelvic organ prolapse is another condition impacting many women, as demonstrated by the 200,000 surgical procedures performed annually in the US to address the problem. [7] Prolapse occurs when pelvic floor musculature and connective tissue are strained and weakened, with inner organs collapsing toward or through the pelvic floor openings. Though women, especially after vaginal deliveries and advanced age, are more prone to the descent of the bladder, uterus, or rectum (through the vagina), men may also suffer from rectal prolapse (through the anus).

Additionally, women suffer a wide range of conditions related to their reproductive or sexual organs. These include endometriosis (an inflammatory disease that can affect the reproductive system); dyspareunia (painful intercourse); vulvodynia (chronic pain around the opening of the vulva often accompanied by burning sensation and irritation); and vaginismus (severe pain and spasms as a result of touch).[8]

When we think of the complexity and location of the pelvis, we begin to understand that other conditions such as tailbone pain; misalignment; back pain; knotted, tight, or weak muscles in the hip, glutes, and pelvis; and sexual dysfunction such as lack of libido, inability to achieve orgasm, and erectile dysfunction in men may also be related to pelvic floor health. (To read more about pelvic floor dysfunction, see Bibliography for recommended reading.)

अहिंसा

HOW DO WE TALK ABOUT PELVIC FLOOR TRAINING?

Healthy pelvic floor muscles support our inner organs by being strong and contractible, and able to open fully, release, and relax. To function optimally, the pelvic floor muscles, like all other muscles, require elasticity. Because of the nature of the area that we are working with, hidden under our clothes and between our legs, the words we use and the instructions we give ourselves are of particular importance. They, too, must be elastic enough to precisely describe the breadth and depth of movement, and to be sensitive, encouraging, and exploratory of *range.*

Let's begin with looking at some of the words commonly used when speaking about pelvic floor training:

KEGELS

In their book, *The Bathroom Key,* Kathryn Kassai and Kim Perelli give an excellent overview of Dr. Kegel's work and his in-depth research on how to help women prevent urinary incontinence. Born in the US in 1894, Dr. Kegel focused on nonsurgical, noninvasive approaches to gynecological problems. When he realized that more than 30% of the women he saw were unable to contract their pelvic floor muscles following a verbal instruction, he invented a pressure sensor that he inserted vaginally, allowing both doctor and patient to see what the patient was doing in a graphic display. Biofeedback is still widely used today, and the contribution of Dr. Kegel, whose name became synonymous with pelvic floor exercises, is undeniably tremendous.[9]

The problem with Kegels arrives after decades of using the word without a real understanding of its meaning, and without making sure that we even know what we are supposed to do. Once in a while a student will get frustrated with my many instructions and metaphors, and they will want to know, "so do I just do a Kegel?!" Most of the time I opt to request that the student forget what they know about Kegels and just drop that word altogether. This decision is not out of a lack of respect for the practice of Kegels, but because, over the years, this word has become a buzzword that translates for most people as, *"just squeeze everything down there as hard as you can."*

In this book I suggest an approach that avoids such repetitions. In fact, such a practice of Kegels can prove counter-effective for many women and even cause hypertense muscles that contribute to pelvic floor dysfunction. How many women have been told to do their Kegels at every stop light? I certainly was. Yet this mechanical work runs counter to the mind-body connection that will yield real healing. We are looking for quality over quantity. That said, if I have a student who is truly attached to the word, no problem. I simply say, "Okay, let's go ahead and do–just a few–*very high-quality* Kegels."

CONTRACTIONS

There is no inherent problem with the word contraction. In fact, we actually want the muscles to be able to *both* contract and release. As with Kegels, the problem is the way the word is understood and translated in the body, especially for beginners. The instruction to contract often yields the quality of a balled-up fist. Something hard and unyielding. Contracting the pelvic floor in such a way for someone who is very tight or weak, or someone who is simply unfamiliar with their pelvic floor muscles (like I was), can be compared to lifting a two-hundred-pound weight without strength, preparation, or technique. You simply can't do it. And if somehow you do, by the power of your will, you are likely to hurt yourself.

One of the reasons I find yoga to be mending is that, in avoiding that hardened quality, we can more easily find movement and a sense of flowing energy that heals. Once a person develops both skill and a deeper understanding of how they use their body, words such as Kegel or contraction will no longer render an automatic, unfruitful response.

SQUEEZING

The term squeezing can also produce just the sort of muscular/mental/emotional tension that we are trying to avoid. Squeezing, gripping, or clenching yields a forceful drawing-in of the vaginal walls for women, and a gripping of the anal sphincter for both sexes. If one is just developing body awareness, the thought of squeezing as if trying to prevent the flow of urine can be useful for the purpose of identifying the area, but not for practicing repetitively, or as the sole means for strengthening.

TIGHTENING

The word tight is often regarded as positive. In this fitness/gym/social media era, people around me continuously strive to look thin and tight. This concept derives from what I conceive as our culture's false, energy-blocking aesthetic outlook. Tightness lacks range, breath, and flow. Deep weakness and inferior range of motion can occur when muscles are too tight.

अहिंसा

ISUF - A RICH & VITAL WAY TO ENGAGE THE PELVIC FLOOR

So, what *can* we say when talking about the pelvic floor? To answer that question, I must revert to my native tongue of Hebrew and explain the wider meaning and connotations of the word I have chosen:

ISUF (איסוף) (ee-soof)

Isuf is a word that perfectly describes the action that we are looking for when engaging the muscles of the pelvic floor. *Isuf* literally means gathering or collecting. And while it can be used for picking scattered papers up off the floor, it is also used in other ways with more subtle qualities that match the quality of movement that we are looking for - a movement of *coming together and lifting*. For example, *isuf* can describe the mindful focus of one's senses when concentrating on a task. It can be used to talk about people coming together and gathering. And *isuf* can describe embracing a child in your arms. You would bend down, gather, embrace, and lift the child, and all of that motion can be expressed and felt from the use of the word *isuf*.

In seeking layers of meaning in body, mind, and heart, I find the concept of *isuf* in all of its richness to be vital for this physical work. *Isuf* works hand in hand with the following concepts that I will introduce: *ahimsa* and *satya.* Like *isuf,* these two words also come from an ancient language–Sanskrit, the language of yoga.

NON-HARMING IN THE FACE OF PAINFUL TRUTH:

The Attitude of *Ahimsa & Satya*

When we think of yoga, complex physical postures may come to mind. But yoga in the Indian tradition is not only about the physical. The seminal Sanskrit yoga text, *Yoga Sutras of Patanjali,*[10] systematically describes how our consciousness functions, while dedicating a mere two lines to yoga postures.

The text puts forth moral directives or restraints regarding how to live with oneself and others. These are the essential pre-requisites for performing postures and breathing exercises. The first of these is *ahimsa*–the practice of non-harming and nonviolence. With *ahimsa* as a guide, we can find within ourselves, and toward ourselves, the strength to act with compassion, kindness, and care. Practicing *ahimsa* means not just avoiding harmful, violent, or aggressive acts, but also avoiding harmful words and thoughts. It means actively protecting and honoring others and ourselves. It means breaking a cycle of pain, shame, and hurtful self-perception. Practicing *ahimsa* is not easy–it is a journey and a process.

In a yoga practice, the simple action of agreeing to lie yourself down on the mat with all vulnerabilities exposed, requires not harming oneself. The first step on your journey of healing rests, therefore, in a commitment to *ahimsa.*

With *ahimsa* as a ground rule, the next essential concept that I wish to introduce from the *Yoga Sutras* is *satya*–truthfulness. Honesty. Sometimes students come to class, and I see that they are overwhelmed by their own vulnerability. Apologetically they tell me stories of the past, how strong and agile and in control of their body they used to be. It is too painful to acknowledge where they are now . . . how their body is now.

"The most fundamental aggression to ourselves, the most fundamental harm we can do to ourselves, is to remain ignorant by not having the courage and the respect to look at ourselves honestly & gently." *Pema Chödrön, When Things Fall Apart*

When facing a painful truth, we must remind ourselves of *ahimsa*–a heart unwilling to do harm, a heart saturated with acceptance. The courageous honesty of *satya* and the open heart of *ahimsa* together cultivate equanimity for whatever comes up in the process of healing. Together they guide us to ignore what does not serve the healing process, such as automatic personal narratives, excuses, or negative thoughts toward oneself and one's body.

Both *ahimsa* and *satya* are qualities that do not come easily, especially when directed inward. They require a great deal of careful attention and inner listening–to our actions, language, and thoughts. Lightheartedness and humor can also greatly help in this regard. In her book on childbirth, the legendary midwife Ina May Gaskin writes:

"I often say that our bottom parts function best when our top part–our minds–are either grateful or amused at the antics or activities of our bottoms. It is amazing how much better our bottoms work when we think of them with humor and affection rather than with terror, revulsion or, worst of all, look away from them in shame. Lord knows, we can't turn our backs on our bottoms." [11]

CULTIVATING *ISUF* WITH SIX TECHNIQUES FOR TRAINING THE PELVIC FLOOR

How can we transition from the theory of *isuf* to the action of *isuf? Isuf* is the coming together of the pelvic floor muscles, and the embracing, and lifting of the perineum. In this section, I will offer six techniques–relax, breathe, look, imagine, move, and feel –for putting *isuf* into action, and for activating the mind-body connection to pelvic floor training.[12] At times, these techniques may feel very distinct from one another, and at other times you may notice them all working simultaneously. On the journey of understanding *how* to create *isuf,* these techniques will function as gateways into focus and control, as entry points to your own healing path.

1] **Relax**–Undo tension in your body

2] **Breathe**–Establish a connection with the breath

3] **Look**–Carefully observe the area you wish to focus on and pay attention to sensation

4] **Imagine**–Create a clear intention of movement and imagine that intention being realized

5] **Move**–Move gently and deliberately

6] **Feel**–Allow for a shift in your physical experience and be present to feel sensations and feelings, physical and emotional

The techniques may be treated as building blocks, one resting upon the other, with you first relaxing, then connecting to your breath, looking and paying attention, imagining your intention of movement, actually moving in a particular manner with a particular quality, and ultimately feeling the physical and emotional sensations that arise as a result. With time, you will see that the techniques are interconnected, and as you become more skilled, you will be able to apply them simultaneously.

RELAX

Pelvic floor disorders are not simple or easy to relax around. When pelvic floor muscles are tight, a high degree of focus and concentration–sometimes over a period of months of practice–is required in order to release them. When there is weakness or lack of muscle tone in the pelvic floor, the larger, more dominant muscles such as the gluteal or abdominal muscles will often jump in to compensate for that weakness. Being able to distinguish whether certain muscles are relaxed or tense is especially important when we intend to engage the pelvic floor muscles, otherwise those larger muscles may be activated *instead.*

In order to recognize where tension is held, and to unravel the tangled layers of tense muscles, sometimes clenched as a self-protective mechanism, relaxing the body is crucial. Practicing in the secure environment of a yoga class, or at home where you feel safe, is vital in order to build trust, let go, and relax. Relaxation in this context is far from doing nothing. It is not a passive or collapsed state but rather an active effort to undo tensions. Relaxation and collapsing are two very different modes of inhabiting our bodies. A state of relaxation comprises a sense of ease, expansion, and softness, while being highly aware of body position and sensation.

Try this

Lie down on your back, legs straight, or bend your knees resting them on a cushion. Imagine sinking pleasantly into the ground. You can imagine warm sand or soft grass beneath you. Surrender the weight of your body, allowing it to be heavy. Scan for any tension you can feel, and then release. When the body is relaxed, you can begin to direct your attention to breathing. When you direct attention to the breath, the body can further relax. Lie here for a few minutes.

Jenny had never done pelvic floor physical therapy when she began practicing yoga with me. In fact, she dreaded anyone coming near her pelvis. For two decades, she suffered pelvic pain, including severe nerve pain that she described as stabbing and sharp, as if needles were poking her in the vaginal area and external genitalia, and dyspareunia, pain with intercourse. "Intercourse feels like you are on fire . . . like someone is holding a flame to your skin." Jenny shared that after her annual visit to the gynecologist, despite the use of a pediatric speculum during the exam, she would suffer for about a week from severe pain accompanied by a bladder infection. She dreaded those appointments. Not too long after joining the pelvic health yoga class, she had her yearly check-up. She told me that when the exam was about to begin, she could hear my voice from class reminding her to relax her buttocks. Along with taking deep expansive breaths, she was able to relax enough for the doctor to use a regular speculum. (A huge deal for her!) The pain following the exam was reduced from the typical week to one day, and no infections followed. In Jenny's case, clenching is a natural, self-protective mechanism. She suffers pelvic pain, anticipates it, fears it, and grips. But finally, with practice, she is able to identify her own resistance, and that alone reduces the pain significantly.

BREATHE

Each minute we breathe in about 12–15 times on average, with air flowing from the outside into our bodies and filling our lungs. Our thoracic cavity expands like an accordion, pushing downward on the belly that, as a result, also expands. With exhalation, the air flows back out of our body into our surroundings, causing a reduction in the size of our trunk as if the bellows of the accordion were squeezed smaller. Though the air moves in and out of the lungs, breathing creates movement in any part of the thoracic and abdominal cavities, and can be felt in other parts of the body as well.[13] From the moment of birth until the moment of death, this process repeats itself ceaselessly.

In yoga, breath itself is an element greater than the physicality of breathing. In yoga, breath is called *prana,* the life force that sustains us. Accompanying *prana* with deep awareness can lead to a profound shift in how we feel ourselves. In this context, utilizing the act of breathing correctly may transform a practice such as pelvic floor training into something intriguing, and dare I say, even spiritual. I once found myself deeply moved when a student, an academic scholar, described breathwork combined with *isuf,* as an internal excavation–implying how deeply intimate, and reaching into unknown terrain, this work can be. The possibility of actually *feeling* the deeper layers of the pelvic floor depends fully on connecting to the breath. The basis of this work is in tracing the change in the shape of your body that expands and widens with inhalation, and softens and narrows with exhalation. Unless otherwise mentioned, in yoga we breathe through the nose.

Try this

Lie down on your back with your knees straight or bent, and put your hands on your belly, so that you can feel your skin–the warmth, texture, and softness of your own body. Breathe slowly and gently toward your hands, feeling the movement of the breath, sweet and nurturing, experiencing the belly as it rises and subsides. Do not draw the breath in or push it out with force, but rather invite the breath inwards and expel it gently.

LOOK

Many of my pelvic health students walk through the door without much experience in yoga. When faced with slow, deliberate movement and the request to turn their gaze inward, they feel impatient. They have made the decision to be proactive about their wellbeing and health, and to give yoga a try, yet still . . . to just lie there, breathe, and relax? In the initial stage of relaxation, we work on releasing any excess tension. But in order to relax more deeply, the distracted, overactive, and anticipating mind needs to focus. We do this through intentional observation–*looking*. When I talk about looking, seeing, and observing, I am not referring to the sense organ of sight–the eyes–but to an inner searching mechanism that feels and takes note of sensation throughout the body, like an internal flashlight.

While looking at a certain area in your body, things may come up such as a memory or an emotion. Allow these thoughts to arise, acknowledge them, and give them space. At the same time, use the physical place you are focusing on in your body as your anchor, observing the sensations (and all that is attached to them) in a nonjudgmental way. This is not always easy. You may observe, for example, that you are holding tension in your inner thighs, or that you are unable to relax your glutes. As a reaction to your observations, you may feel frustrated, angry, fascinated, or disappointed. Allow this range of feeling to be part of the practice.

Try this

Lie down again and, with your mind's eye, *look* at your pelvic region:

The buttocks–Are you clenching?

The sacrum–The triangular area above your tailbone is made up of several vertebrae fused together. Providing support at the base of the spine and connecting to the hip bones, the sacrum is important for pelvic strength and stability. Feel it resting heavily on the ground. Is it tilting to one side?

The groin–Look at the creases between your thighs and belly. Can you feel them deep and soft?

The belly–Look at the lower belly below the navel. Is it warm and soft?

The sitting bones (ischial tuberosities)–Sit up and rock from side to side. Do you feel those pointy bones on both sides of your pelvis? Now lie back down, and hugging your knees to the chest, find those pointy bones with your fingers.

The right sit bone–Lie back down in relaxation and look at the right sit bone and all the soft tissue around it. What do you feel?

The left sit bone–Look at the left sit bone and all the soft tissue around it. What do you see? (You may very well discover that it feels quite different from the opposite side.)

The tailbone (coccyx)–Turn on your side and slide your hand down your spine, pass the sacrum, and touch the very end of this magnificent chain–your tailbone. Now lie back down, close your eyes, and locate your tailbone. How does everything around it feel?

The pubis–The right and left hip bones join at what is termed the *pubic symphysis*. You can feel this pointy bone with your fingers if you slide straight down from the navel. Now relax the body again and with your awareness circle the pubic bone and look at all the soft tissue around it. Observe quietly without judgment, what do you see?

IMAGINE

Imagination is the bridge between observation and action. First we form an intention–a creation of our mind, saturated with awareness. Then we imagine our body fulfilling the intention. This is the seed of *doing*.

When I began teaching focused pelvic health classes I was advised to never guide a person with hypertense pelvic floor muscles to contract their pelvic floor as their muscles were already overly contracted. But over time it became clear to me that, especially for people whose pelvic muscles resist releasing, *imagining* a gentle way in which to engage the muscles is what allows for relaxation to follow. There is no moving and expanding outward without at least the initial intention of moving and collecting inward. It is important to remember that an overly tight muscle is not necessarily a strong muscle.

Similarly, regarding weakness, I remember myself clearly in the year or two after the birth of my son (my second child) trying to contract and lift my pelvic floor while counting till ten, as instructed by the information sheets that I received from nurses, midwives, and doctors. Only when it came time to release the pelvic floor muscles after that supposed long strong contraction, did I realize that there was nothing to relax. It was completely loose already. All that effort, all that squeezing, and there was no tone, no response from my internal muscles. I was exerting so much energy trying to engage an area that I felt no real access to. When I allowed myself to come to my yoga mat with fewer expectations, and to simply set a clear intention and *visualize* where and what needed to move, I was able to feel my body beginning to respond in a way that felt both wholesome and effective. The mind's intent and body's work moved into alignment.

Being intentional with the instructions that you give to the subtle muscles of your pelvic floor is essential. We aim to gain control over what our pelvic floor is doing in order to train it, so that eventually *it will be able to do what it needs to do on its own.* I use the word imagine because we visualize the movement that we eventually want our muscles to perform. When you imagine, you may notice your body respond with actual movement. Don't resist it. If the muscles are not strong or flexible enough to respond with the quality of movement that you imagine, you may experience a kind of choppiness at first. Stay consistent with imagining. Allow body and mind to find one another. We are drawing a map in the body and creating a link between imagination and real response. When that map comes into focus, we can move more clearly and smoothly.

Try this

Lie down, relax, and breathe, just as you did before. Imagine the whole pelvis breathing so that as the lungs, belly, and ribcage expand, so does the entire pelvis. And as all those parts shrink a bit when you exhale, so does the pelvis. Just notice what it is doing and how.

MOVE

When intention is precise, the path for the body is clear. We are ready to move. With the stability of mind that we cultivated by imagining moving, we now anchor the body in one direction and reach toward the other. As we think of both grounding ourselves and expanding out of ourselves, the quality of movement becomes intentional and thoughtful. This idea becomes clear when we talk about postures. For example, if you want to elongate your spine upward as you sit, press the sitting bones into the ground, rooting them gently down.

When moving patiently and deliberately, you should not experience pain. As you familiarize yourself with your pelvic floor and work toward creating the ingathering, lifting movement of *isuf,* stop if you feel tension or discomfort as a result of the movement. Increasing your range of movement with a deeper, stronger contraction and fuller, more complete relaxation requires time and trust. There is no way around that. This is because we are not looking to *imitate* movement. Your body needs to know that your ego will not push you into performing an exercise you are not ready for. Rather, aim for an authentic expression of where and how you are in this moment. I am referring specifically to pelvic floor work, but this principle of patience and trust is true for all the postures and exercises suggested in the next chapter. While the ease and power of other movements can be observed from the outside, with *isuf* only you can feel it. What is special though, is that when you do, your newfound connection and sense of control does shine through.

Try this

Let's build on the imagine exercise and begin to move. Lie down, imagine the whole pelvis breathing, and add this: as you exhale, actively and *very gently* gather-embrace-lift the basket that is the pelvic floor. With the in-breath, let go completely. Take a full breath to rest and repeat.

FEEL

Now that we can direct actual movement inside of us, a subtle sense of expansion reveals itself. This expansion is about finding internal space and a feeling of connectedness. Connecting to bodily sensation, and simply being present to feel it, is healing. In those precious moments when new links are made in the body for the first time, students report feeling whole again, no longer divided or broken. It is through the ability to see the pelvic floor with all of its connections to, and not separate from, the rest of the body, that we get to actually *feel* it. And the pelvic floor . . . wow. . . . It is much more central to our daily life than we care to talk about as a culture. These muscles are responsible for so much–from smoothly emptying our bowels or bladder; to sitting, standing, or walking pain free; to having a satisfying and pleasurable sex life. This allows for a transformation in how we feel ourselves. Once that area feels vivid–lit and alive–its emphasis will naturally diminish as it becomes an organic part of our wonderful self. The feeling technique is about allowing yourself to experience what is happening at a given moment, rather than aiming at an action.

Try this

Now, in whatever position you are in, notice any sensations and emotions that arise and stay present to feel them.

Find different moments throughout your day when you can tune into feeling and sensation:
When you are eating . . . can you feel the textures in your mouth and really taste the flavors of your food?
When you are driving . . . can you feel your shoulders? Is there tension? Can you relax them?
When you are brushing your teeth . . . can you notice how it feels on your gums?
When you prepare your morning coffee . . . can you feel how the aroma affects your body?
When you hear a child's laughter or indulge in the cuteness of a beloved pet . . . where in your body do you feel joy? In your cheeks because you are smiling? In an expansion in your chest?
When you stand barefoot on a wooden floor, cold tile, grass, water, or sand . . . how do your feet respond? Do your toes squeeze, do they spread out? Does that sensation echo in other areas of the body?
When you are sad . . . where in your body is that sensation located?
When you are outside . . . can you notice how your skin feels, say, in the sun or in the wind?

Sandra

After class one day, Sandra shared with me that, "Now I have mini revelations in every class. Sometimes it's not so much something new, but almost a brief moment where there is a more definitive connection. And I know that there are more moments to come where I will feel more of these connections."

Sandra is in her thirties and joined my pelvic health classes with chronic pain in the lower abdominal area that included constant cramping and sometimes stabbing pains. She had hip surgery a few years earlier and is not certain about what caused the pain that led her into surgery (traumatic injuries from cheerleading and triathlons did not help), but has been suffering chronic constipation, lower back pain, hip joint pain, pain during intercourse, and difficulty emptying the bladder for years. For Sandra, who for so long felt in pieces, to feel a sense of connectedness in her body is a major transformation.

BE GENTLE WITH YOURSELF

A few years ago, at the end of a three-week-long yoga retreat with master teacher Orit Sen Gupta, she told me that it seemed as if I hear her instructions in a "higher volume" than intended. Reflecting on this conversation, I acknowledge the truth in that, the truth in how "good" I try to be, how "perfect" in execution. The journey and process of healing my own pelvic floor disorder has taught me so much about myself, yoga, and life. And about the delicacy that this particular practice requires–the gentleness.

And so, it is important to me now to take this extra moment. Please allow yourself to be playful and creative; to be gentle with yourself when going through this process of learning how to approach your pelvic floor. Listen to the voice inside you without the need to prove anything to it, or to the world, when trying out the exercises. Do a little less, listen a little more, and trust in your innate ability to heal, perhaps in unexpected ways.

ISUF IN ACTION:

Fundamental Exercises for Training the Pelvic Floor

Now that you have been introduced to some anatomy and the techniques, you are ready to look for your *isuf*—a nuanced, sometimes delicate, sometimes powerful, gathering and lifting of the pelvic floor. You are also ready to find *your* release—a sense of openness and softness within the pelvis.

It is important to remember that the body, and its muscles and connective tissue, need to adjust and get stronger and more elastic *over time.* Therefore, you may need to spend several weeks simply imagining some of the following exercises before the body will catch up with the mind. Sometimes it may be the reverse and your body may be ready but you find it hard to concentrate or feel foggy when trying to access those muscles. Stay patiently consistent while nurturing the mind-body connection.

These exercises are not intended to be taken on as a strict, daily regime. Explore them, try a couple of them one day, then a couple of others another day, and slowly build awareness and muscular tone to support executing them correctly, with smooth and controlled internal movement. You will notice that *isuf* is always led by the exhalation, breathing the air out. And the release, counter to how many people feel is intuitive for them, happens on the in-breath, inhalation. Note that, eventually, when these actions become natural to you, you will not have to worry about your pattern of breathing. But as you learn to train your pelvic floor, stick to this pattern of breath as it will yield the desired result in your body.

Coordinated Breathing

Stand up or come to a comfortable seated position with your spine long. Find ease in the body and observe your breath. Look, observing the perineum from within, and imagine that it is being lifted in coordination with the exhalation. When you breathe in, the perineum moves gently down. After a few rounds of breath, use your exhale to lift the perineum towards the belly more actively. On each in-breath make sure to relax. As you breathe for a few minutes through this practice, connect to feeling the movement in the pelvic floor, subtle as it may be. **Practice for 3–5 minutes.**

This can be tricky! Often students will ask, "Wait, aren't I supposed to relax when I exhale?" And the person asking will slouch as they say the word "relax." The arrival of exhalation carries with it a tremendous opportunity to relax further and let go. Yet emptying the body of air *also* allows for the entire core system to feel most compact. Without the pressure of the filled-up lungs and the respiratory diaphragm moving downward, there is more internal space to lift up the whole pelvic floor. With time, you will want to be able to engage the pelvic floor when breathing naturally, regardless if you are inhaling or exhaling, but for the purpose of training and understanding the movement of *isuf*, this pattern is essential.

Mirroring

Diaphragm & Pelvic Floor

Think of the pelvic floor as mirroring the diaphragm–the main respiratory muscle, shaped like a dome, that separates the thoracic (ribs and chest) cavity from the abdominal cavity. As you inhale, the diaphragm moves down. As you exhale it relaxes and floats upward.

Stand up or come to a comfortable seated position with your spine long. Imagine how the pelvic floor and diaphragm mirror each other and are reflected in one another. On the inhale feel them both move down; on the exhale feel them both move up.
Practice for 3–5 minutes.

Ribs & Pelvis

Stand up or lie down on your back and place your hands on your rib cage. As the ribs expand outward with the inhalation, look for that same quality reflecting in the pelvis. Imagine that the bellows of the accordion exist in the pelvis as well. With the outbreath, observe how both the ribs and the pelvis become more compact, as if the accordion is being squeezed inwards. Ribs and pelvis–both move out, both move in. **Practice for 3–5 minutes.**

The Hammock

Stand up or come to a comfortable seated position with your spine long, and place your hands on your belly below the navel. Relax the body and focus on your breath. Imagine the pelvic floor hanging at the base of your pelvis from front to back, suspended like a hammock. Now imagine the breath as a thick, liquid energy flowing and pouring into the pelvic region. With the gentle expanding of the lower belly on the inhale, feel the hammock filling with the weight of your breath. On the exhale, the hammock becomes lighter and floats up towards your belly.
Practice for 3–5 minutes.

The Diamond and its Four Corners

Lie down on your back and relax your body. Breathe in and imagine the four corners of the pelvic floor (the right sitting bone, left sitting bone, pubic bone, and tailbone) moving away from one another and expanding like a yawn. Breathe out and imagine all four corners moving closer to each other and gathering inwards in *isuf*. Gradually your imagination becomes real movement, smooth and precise. **Practice for 3–5 minutes.**

Sphincters

The sphincters are circular, ring-like muscles, responsible for regulating the closing and opening of bodily passages. We have many sphincters, including in our eyes, throat, heart, and digestive system. Here we are mostly concerned with our lower sphincters–the anal sphincter located at the end of the rectum and the urethral sphincter in charge of the passage of urine. Both sphincters have two rings, internal and external. However, we can only voluntarily control the external sphincters. Women, in addition, have a vaginal sphincter. When the sphincters do not function properly, and if the muscles are too weak or too contracted, symptoms such as lack of control over urine or feces occur.

While our practice will focus on these three (two for men) bottom openings, paying attention to the ring muscle of the mouth is important. There is a fascinating early embryo connection between the ring muscle of the mouth and the bottom openings. Around day fifteen in the creation of an embryo, two depressions form: one becomes the oropharyngeal membrane that eventually forms the mouth, and the other becomes the cloacal membrane that eventually forms the openings of the urinary, reproductive, and digestive tracts. Even as the spine develops, they remain connected.[14] In this context, the awareness itself of this connection is valuable.

The Rings

Anus: Lie down on your back or come to a comfortable seated position with your spine long. Inhale, allow the anus to softly expand as if (just imagine) the ring can become wider. Exhale, create a suction-type feeling from deep within the rectum resulting in a gradual contraction of the anus. Inhale, relax the anal sphincter; exhale, feel the ring becoming tighter and more compact. **Repeat 3–5 times.**

Vagina: Lie down on your back or come to a comfortable seated position with the spine long. Inhale, allowing the vagina to feel as if it is broadening both at the opening as well as from within. Exhale, visualize the vaginal walls moving inwards as if creating a narrower pathway. The movement of the ring is even from all directions and in coordination with the breath. **Repeat 3–5 times.**

Urethra: Lie down on your back or come to a comfortable seated position with your spine long. Inhale, imagine the urethra as a tube, widening and elongating. Exhale, now imagine it shortening, with an inward, suction-like movement. **Repeat 3–5 times.**

Years ago, in an open conversation with a male colleague and dear friend, I learned that a trick that I thought was my own, he, as a thorough and curious yoga teacher, had experimented with as well. In order to work with the front part of the pelvic floor, the urethra, we have both found it useful to imagine possessing the opposite sex's genitalia. I confessed that it was incredibly helpful to imagine as if a penis were elongating itself out of my body with the inhalation, and then as if it were shrinking inwards with the exhalation. He, in turn, shared that in order to access these muscles in a deeper way, he tried to visualize how the penis may collect inwards as if it were a vagina. Something in this practice allows for a real increase in the range of movement!

The Vocal Ring

The first time I truly experienced in my body the deep connection between the mouth (and jaw) and the pelvic floor was during the birth of my daughter. In order to cope with the intensity of labor, I repeated the sound AUM focusing on allowing the vibration of the sound to impact the opening of the cervix. At some point, the sound spontaneously shifted into a louder, soothing, singing sound. When that wasn't sufficient, I recalled Ina May Gaskin's suggestion in her books to kiss my partner with an open and soft mouth between contractions. The effect on dilation was immediate.

Ina May calls this phenomena Sphincter Law, and though she is speaking about giving birth, I find her conclusions very relevant to anything relating to the pelvic floor—from elimination to sex, for women and for men. She writes: "Excretory, cervical, and vaginal sphincters function best in an atmosphere of intimacy and privacy. . . . These sphincters cannot be opened at will and do not respond well to commands. . . When a person's sphincter is in the process of opening, it may suddenly close down if that person becomes upset, frightened, humiliated, or self-conscious. . . . The state of relaxation of the mouth and jaw is directly correlated to the ability of the cervix, the vagina, and the anus to open to full capacity." When we acknowledge the pelvic-jaw connection while working to increase pelvic floor health, we begin to realize how these two areas influence one another. Many students report feeling tension in the jaw, but are then able to consciously relax the mouth and notice the pelvic floor echo that relaxation, and vice versa.

AUM

Come to a comfortable seated position with your spine long. As you create the following sounds, feel the vibration moving deep into your body, particularly the pelvis.

~ Inhale deeply, exhale with the sound A (aah . . .)

~ Inhale deeply, exhale with the sound U (ooh . . .)

~ Inhale deeply, exhale with the sound M (mm . . .)

~ Inhale deeply, exhale, and make the full sound of AUM moving from an open mouth to gradually closing it.

Repeat the four sounds for a second round. Create intention to feel a delicate *isuf* accompanying the sound. The sound in itself can be thought of as a gentle weight placed on the pelvic floor, adding more resistance to work with.

The Pebble

Chose one of the following positions: Lie down on your back, come to a comfortable seated position with the spine long, or stand up. (I recommend you try this exercise in all three positions.) The spine is long and the body at ease. Imagine that right at the center of your pelvic floor at the perineum, rests a small, smooth river pebble (or a flower, or whatever visual image works for you!). Inhale and relax. Exhale, as the four corners of the pelvic floor (see Diamond exercise) move inwards, collect the pebble, and lift it upwards towards the belly. Inhale, the four corners move out and the pebble slides out. (A sensation of gliding out is equally important to that of drawing in and lifting.) **Repeat 3–5 times.**

If you know that you suffer from tightness in the pelvic floor, or if you notice that you do through these exercises, keep the *isuf* part in the realm of imagining, and emphasize the letting go of the pebble so that the muscles may find expansion and relax. Similarly, if your muscles lack tone, take care not to overdo the relaxation. The pebble is released; it is not *pushed* out. Accentuate the muscles moving to find the pebble and lift it up.

The Pebble and the Pearl

Lie down on your back with your knees bent and feet parallel on the ground at hip-width apart. Place your hands on your ribs. Breathe in deeply, focus on the expansion of the rib cage. Exhale, observe the ribs moving closer to each other. Imagine that you are holding a precious jewel, a pearl perhaps, in the space between the ribs just beneath the sternum. As you inhale and expand sideways, can you maintain that pearl safely nestled in your body?

Let's go back to *isuf.* Inhale and relax. Exhale, find the pebble and lift it energetically up to meet the pearl. The pearl, too, extends itself gently to meet the pebble. Inhale and relax fully; the ribcage expands and the pelvic floor releases. I call this the *pebble-pearl connection.* **Repeat 3–5 times.**

When this connection is clear to you, try these breaths while sitting and standing.

The Elevator

Come to a comfortable seated position with your spine long. Imagine your pelvis as a building with several "floors." The very base of the pelvis is the "ground floor," a little higher up is the "first floor," and a little higher yet is the "second floor." An elevator moves up and down right through the center, carrying the pebble.

Once you are able to visualize the "floors" in a seated position, lie down on your back, your legs stretched out, hands on your ribs. Take a couple of deep breaths and relax. Inhale. Exhale and collect the pebble at the "ground floor." Hold it there and take a short breath in. Exhale and lift the pebble up only to the "first floor." Hold it there and take a short breath in. Exhale and lift the pebble to the "second floor." Inhale and imagine the elevator moving all the way back to the "ground floor." Take several long deep breaths and release your pelvic floor. **Repeat 1–3 times.**

Note that to execute this practice, a good degree of body awareness and muscular control is required. Have patience with yourself, as it may take a couple months of repeating the previous practices before you can feel this one. When this practice becomes clear in your body, try it both sitting and standing up.

अहिंसा

NURTURING PELVIC HEALTH
YOGA PRACTICES & PERSONAL STORIES

ALIGNMENT

There is a certain way that our body is meant to be stacked and organized, and for our joints to be placed in relation to one another and to gravity, in order to allow optimal function and a healthy blood, neurological, and lymphatic flow. Ideally, if we look at the vertical position, the hips should be directly over the knees and ankles, and the torso directly over the hips, with the head reaching up. When the skeleton is aligned along this weight-bearing axis, structural support is maximized, bone strength increased, and degeneration of joints is prevented.[16] In her book *Alignment Matters,* Katy Bowman writes "To isolate parts of the body when strengthening or to think of strength as something any less than a whole-body event is to miss the point."[17] So when we ask–*Why do I actually need all of these yoga postures when I really just need to strengthen my pelvic floor? Why is alignment really that important, and what does my neck have to do with my bladder anyway?*–we are missing the point of the pelvic floor existing in the context of our whole body. After we turn on our "internal flashlight," and learn to identify and feel what our pelvic floor is, and what *isuf* is and what it feels like, we are ready to treat and work on the whole system. In yoga we place ourselves in different positions–yoga postures *(asana)*–and within these positions, we carefully look at our alignment and strive for a structure that will allow the least friction and most freedom and flow. I love the word energy and use it in my classes all the time, but really, we are talking about rejuvenation on a cellular level, a flow that is very physical indeed.

While we strive to find alignment, we must remember that the way we stand, sit, walk, and drive all affect bodily alignment. We are right- or left-handed; we stand with more weight on our heels or toes, or with more weight on one foot or the other, along with many more habits of movement and posture. Living in the world, we do not remain in the perfect state of babyhood. We slip, fall, suffer injury, and get challenged over and over again–physically, mentally, and emotionally. All of this affects our body. And we are not symmetrical; we will never be symmetrical. Alignment is not perfection; it is a continuous search saturated with awareness, at once adaptable and forgiving.

TRANSFORMATION THROUGH PRACTICE

To transform our alignment and the way we move, even in the most delicate of ways, practice is key. In our practice, we do not seek to imitate an imagined state of symmetry and perfection. There is no quick fix, no transference of responsibility. This is not to say that we do not need doctors, nurses, holistic practitioners, nutritionists, etc. But for a process to really belong to us, to become a part of us, practicing is vital. Through the practice of yoga *asana,* we can find healthy alignment that rests on our musculoskeletal structure, a balanced distribution of weight, and an awareness of how we carry ourselves throughout our day. Indeed, developing awareness of alignment is an important steppingstone on the path to healing pelvic floor disorders. Growing our agility, building strength and finding stability from within, all contribute to an expanding perception of self and our overall health as human beings inhabiting our bodies to the utmost.

As you work with the practices outlined below, think of the process as slowly and patiently sketching a map within your body, making connections that will guide your whole body to work toward greater pelvic health. I suggest being both committed and playful in your approach to practicing. There are a few ways you can go about it. Choose a sequence of four to five exercises to do daily. (Different ideas for flowing practices will follow this chapter along with the option to listen to a recorded version.) If you practice two or three times a week, that is fine too. If you have more time and can go through all of the asanas in the order presented, great. The most important thing is listening to your body. Doing more and working "harder" is not better in this case. If you are uncomfortable with one of the postures, it is okay in this context to simply skip it and revisit it when you have face-to-face guidance from a skilled yoga teacher. This practice is not meant to replace your yoga practice or favorite workout. Approach each exercise from the standpoint of maintaining awareness of breath, alignment, and what you feel is happening in your pelvis and pelvic floor. Whether working on your core, stretching, or performing a breathing exercise, ask yourself: Am I sagging? Am I clenching? Am I contracted on only one side? Can I find and connect to an organic, pulsating feeling of *isuf* and its gentle release, in every movement and practice?

PERSONAL STORIES

My students are the heart and soul of this book. Their insights and stories of healing—morsels of which they oftentimes share with me at the end of class, and sometimes in an excited text or email—sustain me with joy, and reinforce and help me refine my work. The stories you will read have been generously shared by students who participated regularly in my Yoga for Pelvic Floor Health group classes or who took private lessons on a regular basis. They are stories of women and men of different ages and wide-ranging professions. In the stories, my students refer to the Yoga for Pelvic Floor Health class as yoga, pelvic floor yoga, and other such titles, all talking about the same method.

The stories appear alongside the yoga practices that I associate with the healing process of the storyteller. Keywords at the beginning of each story point to the challenges that these students faced, and the elements that helped them find a path to healing. Names have been changed to protect privacy.

Katelyn

Postpartum ~ Prolapse ~ Anxiety ~ Visualization ~ Relaxation

If you would have told me a couple of years ago that I would be doing yoga on a regular basis, I would have laughed. The idea of sitting still or staying in a pose didn't appeal to me. If I wasn't doing fast and high-intensity movements, I didn't feel like I was doing much for my body. After the birth of my first child at the age of 31, my outlook on working out and my body changed.

At four weeks postpartum I knew something was wrong. Physically, I felt off, with a heaviness and dragging in my vagina like I was sitting on a rubber ball. After too much googling and many tears, my OBGYN reassured me that this was all "normal postpartum," and that I just needed to wait it out and do my Kegels. I had the doctor check internally while I did a Kegel to make sure I was doing it correctly, and she told me that I was, and that I had a little prolapse that would probably go away on its own. "Probably" was not good enough for me, and I requested a referral for physical therapy, which she gave me reluctantly. There I received the official prolapse diagnosis I was dreading. I felt broken. I had been brought up to believe that women's bodies would "just naturally know what to do." I felt mine had failed me. I was physically uncomfortable, horrified by the idea of my internal organs sagging out, and depressed. My physical therapist helped me discover problem areas I never even knew existed, and that I actually couldn't hold a Kegel if I tried. I cried about the exercise list of "don't dos" for prolapse, like no jumping or heavy lifting, and I thought I would never get my body back. That's when she handed me a flyer for Leah's pelvic floor yoga class and everything changed.

The first class was a lot of relaxation, meditation, and breathing. As a notoriously anxious person, these are all things that I am not good at. Although I "relax" sometimes when I am at home, the guided relaxation in class made me realize that I had never felt relaxation to that degree. My body was always on alert and I had never breathed fully or felt breath and relaxation travel through my body before. The gentle guidance helped me feel like my body wasn't working against me anymore.

After a few classes I was frustrated that I couldn't get my pelvic floor to move in the way I thought it should but the visualizations were so helpful. Leah would say to imagine your pelvic floor could move in a certain way even if you don't feel it yet. I would imagine keeping my pearl close, lifting the pebble, and just being able to move my stubborn muscles. After a couple of months of visualization, when I finally felt my pelvic floor move as a whole in the way I had envisioned, it was the most eye-opening experience for me, and for the first time my body felt connected. Even simple alignment adjustments made all the difference for me. My pelvis moves ever so slightly into position and it's like I'm putting a puzzle piece back into place and working muscles long forgotten.

By one year postpartum, my daily symptoms of prolapse disappeared. A mild prolapse is still there, but yoga helps me keep my symptoms at bay. I came to yoga to help with my prolapse, yet it has brought so much more to my life. I feel stronger in mind and body now than I did pre-baby. Now, eight months postpartum the second time around, I can say that there is life after a prolapse diagnosis, and yoga has helped me to get that life back.

सत्य

Savasana - Relaxation

Releases tension, calms the mind, allows for vulnerability

Relaxation is traditionally practiced at the end of yoga class, but here we will also start our practice with relaxation to release excess tension before beginning to move. We lie down in stillness, let go, and rest. *Savasana* means corpse pose in Sanskrit. In the ancient Hindu tradition from which the name is drawn, death is a time of transformation. *Savasana* in this context is undoing tension, judgment, and active reflections to allow a deeper process to transpire, to allow an internal, transformative shift in how we are.

Lie down on your back with your legs straight. If you experience any tension in your lower back, modify by placing a cushion under your knees. Rest the arms alongside your body with the palms of the hands facing up. Find stillness, close your eyes, and release your breath. Scan your body from top to bottom and bottom to top, allowing all parts of the body to soften into the ground. If you wish, **set a timer for 5–10 minutes.**

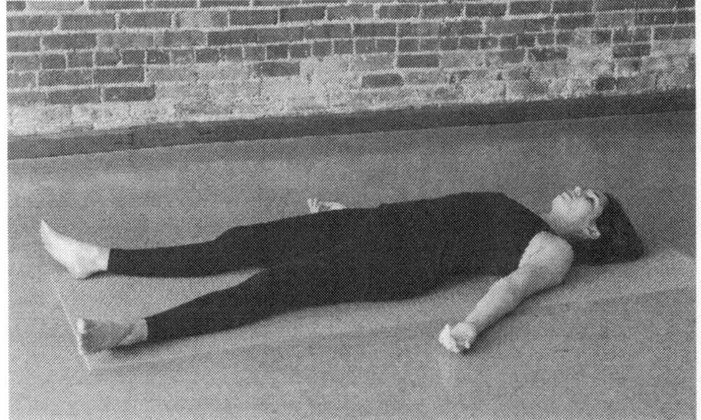

Neutral Spine

What is a neutral spine?

A neutral spine maintains the natural curves of the cervical, thoracic, and lumbar spine. We do not try to flatten out the curve of the neck or lower back, nor do we forcefully tuck the tailbone under in order to be "straight."

Shea

Sexual trauma ~ PTSD ~ Vaginismus ~ Trust ~ Rooting the feet

As a survivor of childhood sexual abuse and trauma, my road to recovery has been painful. Along with ulcerative colitis and posttraumatic stress disorder (PTSD), I was also diagnosed with vaginismus (feels like a panic attack in the vagina), which made penetration during intercourse unbearable. It felt as if I was being stabbed internally with a knife with alcohol being poured on the wound. I went to a sex therapist for years before finally admitting that I was an alcoholic and that drinking made sex possible. When I got sober, the real work began.

The body memories surfaced constantly. I tried yoga, but every time I would go to class I would have panic attacks and flashbacks as I moved through the postures, and I cried through most classes. My body wanted to move, but it was just so painful. I spent a lot of time in child's pose or corpse pose to calm down. The panic attacks coupled with the anxiety I felt by being around other people as this happened was overwhelming, so I started walking on trails in the woods. This way I was able to move as slowly as I needed without the external stimulus of others. I knew the next step was to find a yoga instructor who I could trust as I worked through all of the body triggers and memories.

By the time I started working with Leah privately, my posture felt crippling. We began slowly unwinding my body from having been in a clenched fight-or-flight position my entire life. My core and pelvic floor both terrified me, so I had just ignored them for years. I wanted the midsection of my body to be removed so I didn't have to deal with it. I was so angry when I first started yoga. I wanted my body to move like "normal people." Eventually the panic attacks and crying stopped. For so long, my movements were fragmented with no connection to the body as a whole. It was as if each appendage was its own island, isolated from the others. It's very confusing to have a body that feels like it is just in pieces. Yoga has helped me integrate them. Very slowly, my core began to engage and my body started working "in concert" (as Leah likes to say).

She gives me images to use—like spreading my toes in the mud with deep roots like a cypress tree—to enable shifts that need to occur in my body. Working with the pelvic floor I visualize pulling a corset tight as I protect a tiny, precious pearl in the center of my body. This visualization helps me, as I find the rhythm of letting go in some areas while simultaneously resisting in others. Healing isn't linear. I believe that we are only able to help others to the degree that we are willing to heal ourselves. I am a massage therapist and a certified trauma touch therapist, and I am grateful to have a profession where I can continue to pass the healing on. It's all connected.

सत्य

Our Deep Core Muscles Work Together

The transverse abdominal muscles are the deepest layer of abdominals; they wrap around the trunk of the body from the sternum and pubis in the front, attaching around the back to the spine. They are connected to the pelvic floor muscles in the front, and are therefore especially important to strengthen in harmony with the entire deep core system of the pelvic floor, spinal muscles, and respiratory diaphragm. The activation of the internal obliques, and the transversus abdominis in particular, contributes to the ability to perform a strong pelvic floor contraction.[18] The pelvic floor collaborates with these muscles to create a powerful corset supporting the body all around *and* from below.

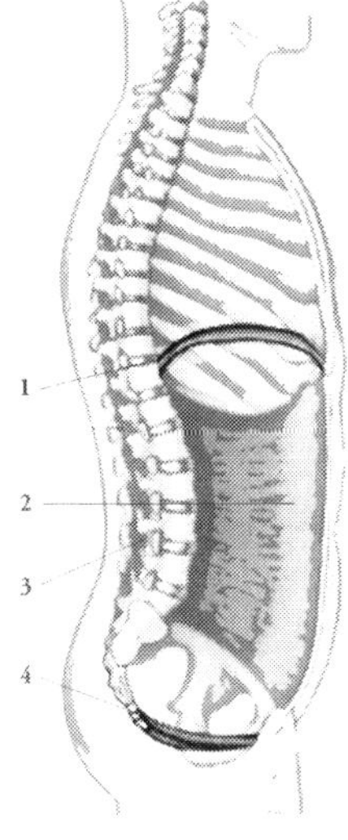

1 Diaphragm
2 Transversus abdominis
3 Multifidus
4 Muscles of pelvic floor

We do not want the pelvic floor to compensate for a weak back, abdominals, glutes, or legs. Nor do we want the pelvic floor to be ignored and slack while other supporting muscles are working overtime.

While activating the abdominals does not necessarily result in the activation of the pelvic floor, *isuf* does trigger the activation of the transversus abdominis. Pay attention to the coordination of your deep core system as you move, going as slowly and softly as you need.

Squeezing and Releasing a Block

Strengthens coordination between inner thighs, transversus abdominis, pelvic floor, and breath

Lie down on your back with your knees bent and feet hip-width apart and parallel. The spine is neutral. Place a yoga block, squishy ball, or folded blanket between your knees. Inhale deeply while expanding the ribcage. Exhale, and squeeze the block while your deep abdominal muscles engage like a corset around your body. With the next in-breath, release the pressure on the block and allow your ribs to expand. On your next exhale, as you squeeze the block, add *isuf*. To fine-tune the practice, pay attention that you do not squeeze your glutes or tilt the pelvis. **Repeat 5–8 times.**

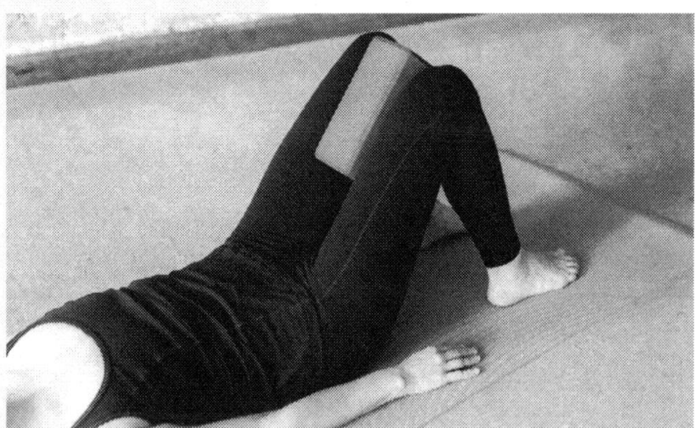

Pelvic-Rib Connection

In my interview with Sandra, she tells me she always loved yoga and when she finally had to give that up, as she had given up other physical activities due to injuries and chronic pelvic pain, it was a great loss. "But," she says, reflecting, "I had been practicing it all wrong. . . . Poses that looked impressive externally didn't feel good from the inside. The days I can get into poses and feel my ribs move–those are the days I feel so good." When I first saw Sandra in class, I was puzzled. Her range of motion was quite extensive yet limited by pain. She stood tall but felt locked. I noticed that there was barely any movement in her rib cage when she breathed. While her abdominals would inflate on the inhale, it was virtually impossible for her to direct the breath to expand the ribs. Even though she came to yoga to help with her pelvic issues, it was quickly apparent that without the ability to soften the rib cage and find a way for it to expand and contract, the pelvis would remain reluctant to respond as well.

While Sandra was struggling with hypertense muscles, my student Andrea was working toward finding tone in the pelvic floor. Her tendency was to stand with her ribs pushed out in the front, abdominals underneath the ribs contracting forcefully, her buttocks pushed out behind and clenched. Andrea works out and would be considered very fit. Yet her ribcage being out of alignment was inhibiting her from finding her deep core strength not from the top of the abdominals but all the way from the bottom–from the pelvic floor. In order for the base of the pelvis to engage, the front ribs must relax.

I see it like this: When we lift the ribs, it is as if we communicate lack of trust in the power of the pelvic floor. The ribs are thrusting out trying to "help" the pelvic floor lift. Once the ribs learn to soften, allowing the abdominal muscles to engage, the message sent to the perineum is one of trust. This allows a connection between the abdominal-pelvic cavity and the thoracic cavity.

Andrea (told by Leah)

Urine leakage ~ Lack of sensation in sex ~ Pregnancy and birth ~ Visualization

Andrea experienced a birth injury with her first daughter. She tells me that her perineum was so torn and swollen that the stiches needed to be redone three days after the birth. But it wasn't until after her second delivery four years later that symptoms of pelvic floor dysfunction led her to seek help. A partial bladder prolapse and urine leakage bothered her, but it was the lack of tone and loss of sensation during sex that frustrated Andrea the most. Her physical therapist explained to her that her muscle tone was in the "back" (where her Kegels were directed) and that she needed to work on strengthening the "front." Andrea recounts how she felt superficially strong, she worked out, did her Kegels, and rode her bike, but her symptoms were not improving. When Andrea's pregnancy at the time ended in miscarriage, she looked for a less medicalized environment in which she could rebuild her strength, both physically and emotionally.

From the first moment she stepped into the yoga studio I enjoyed her presence, curiosity, and commitment. She was always excited to share what images worked well for her body, allowing her to dive deeper into her practice. "After just one class I felt a difference. Visualizations helped me tap into the varied muscle groups involved in the pelvic floor. I realized I had been using my strong glutes, thighs, and upper abs to cheat on my exercises and that I wasn't using my core properly." Her newfound understanding of how to engage her ribs with relation to what was happening in the lower region of her body, and how to incorporate breathing, was of particular importance. "Now I have everything working together. No one muscle group takes over while the others are on vacation. I had trouble breathing to the extent that I thought I had asthma, but now I've learned how to exhale, and that if I do not exhale properly it prevents me from strengthening my lower abs." When I interview Andrea, she shares that she feels a real difference in her sex life as well, with more control and sensation during intercourse. It is my favorite part when she exclaims, "I feel alive." Andrea describes yoga as being a meaningful self-care experience, one that emphasizes feelings of strength and healing, rather than restriction or dysfunction.

When she got pregnant again, she bought a triangular-shaped wedge to place under her back so she could comfortably do the exercises, and she kept coming to class until she had the beautiful homebirth she wanted. Often women ask me if these exercises are safe for pregnancy and the answer is ***yes****. Modifications are needed when it isn't comfortable to lie on one's back; lying on the belly is replaced with exercises on all fours; and if ever an exercise does not feel right, that should be modified as well. The class, as it turned out, benefited Andrea's birthing experience. She reported feeling her pelvic floor muscles engage in a different way than in her two previous births, and an ability to both push–and relax–when needed.*

सत्य

Supta badha konasana - reclining bound angle pose: open & close

Stabilizes pelvis and ribs; strengthens the inner thighs, transverse abdominis, and pelvic floor

Lie down on your back with your knees bent and inner thighs touching. The feet are close together on the ground. Inhale, open the knees away from one another, and allow the groin to relax. Exhale, ground your feet, and lift the knees back together while practicing *isuf*. As you open and close your knees, maintain a neutral spine and a stable pelvis. To fine-tune your practice, observe the deep core system working in unison.

Repeat 5–8 times.

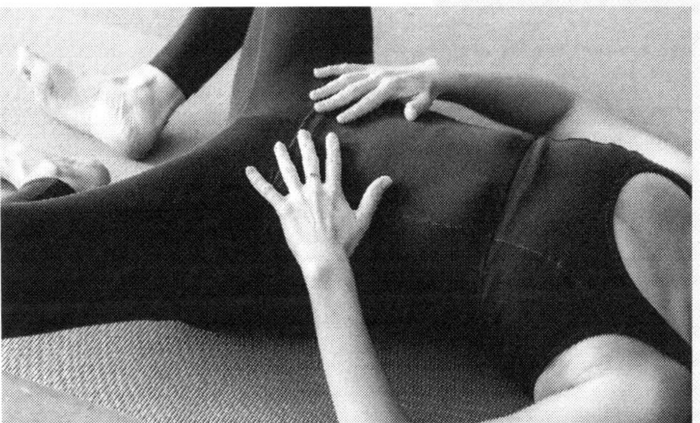

Raakel

Fecal incontinence ~ Shame ~ Doubt ~ Compassion ~ Breath

Yoga for pelvic floor health is just what I needed to deal with my challenge, which is fecal incontinence—uncontrolled leakage of stool. It began in my mid-thirties, probably as a result of a difficult childbirth, but has persisted and worsened over the years. (I am sixty-seven now.)

Fecal incontinence has affected my life in many ways. I liked to run for exercise and the fun of local races, but my bouts of stool leakage interfered. I used menstrual pads of all sizes and kinds and worried that people could smell the leakage. Eventually, I gave up running, but that did not end my problem. I continued to have leakage and gas while walking, and at unexpected and unpredictable times. My sex life with my husband was fraught with worry about what might happen if I lost control during an intimate situation. I felt frustrated and depressed. And it wasn't like having knee pain because I couldn't discuss this with anyone—not friends, not family. I tried so many things over the years, including prescription and over-the-counter medication, biofeedback training to strengthen my anal sphincter muscles, and even a device to block my stool, but nothing solved the problem.

Finally, I was referred to a physical therapist who used a method for relaxation of the pelvic floor muscles (mine were too tight most of the time) followed by gentle contractions. She then had me coordinate these movements with proper breathing. I found this hard to do, and was skeptical that this approach would help me. However, I was astounded to discover that this therapeutic approach worked wonders! After twenty years of living with this issue, I was seeing success. I went from having bowel issues almost daily to rarely having an issue, even during strenuous and long activities such as day hikes through the mountains. Wow!

My physical therapist taught me a few other useful things like how to control the consistency of my stool using psyllium and diet, and how to use proper defecation techniques (such as a footstool to elevate my legs, as well as breathing techniques). Through this therapist, I found my pelvic health yoga class. In yoga we learn to relax our pelvic floor muscles and breathe, and then how to gently contract our muscles while breathing. For years, it seemed, I had been doing everything backwards, and it took a lot of concentration to do the exercises correctly and coordinate my breathing. We are always encouraged to begin where we can and do as much as we can even if our pace is different than that of others. One of the best things about yoga is that it motivates me to continue improving and practicing throughout the day, as I ride in the car or when I'm fixing lunch.

Not everything we do in class is easy for me. Sometimes it is overwhelming to try to do everything Leah describes. But, in the very first class, she introduced us to the concept of compassion—not necessarily just for others but also for ourselves. I return to this thought often, telling myself that if I can't perform the exercises the way I want to, I should allow myself to relax and try again, and not let my inner voice criticize myself. After a couple of months, I was excited to discover that after a 30-minute session of pelvic floor muscle control exercises, my pelvic floor actually felt warm. The muscles were working. I felt proud that I was making progress.

*I have always felt that I needed more core strength, but never knew how to achieve this. In yoga I am learning that when I stabilize my pelvis and keep my spine long, it is easier to increase abdominal strength and for the muscles of my pelvic floor to respond correctly. I feel that as I age, without the support of yoga, incontinence could once again become problematic because my muscles might revert to the poor condition, tightness, and lack of coordination that contributed to my problem. Emotionally I feel that I am improving every time I practice, and that makes me happy. It took me over twenty years, but I am now almost without instances of fecal incontinence. So I would like to say to anyone with this or a similar problem–**Do not give up !***

सत्य

90 degrees

Strengthens legs, rectus abdominis, transverse abdominis, back, pelvic floor

Lie down on your back and raise your legs toward the sky, then bend your knees at a 90-degree angle. Push your hands straight into the thighs and simultaneously push your thighs into your hands. Implement the *pebble–pearl* connection (see Exercises for Training the Pelvic Floor). Hold for about 10 counts (try counting aloud) while breathing naturally. Rest. **Repeat 1–3 times.**

Loren

Back injury ~ Pain and numbness ~ Incontinence ~ Repatterning

I am first and foremost a mover. After a professional dance career, I pursued an MFA in dance performance. During my first year as a graduate student, I woke up one day with no feeling down the right side of my body from the waist down. I had ruptured two discs at L4/L5 and L5/S1. The MRI also showed spondylolisthesis (lower vertebrae slipping forward). The three neurosurgeons I sought advice from varied in opinion from "yes to both surgeries" to "just get one!" to "you don't need surgery at all." My symptoms continued after no intervention: numbness and/or tingling down the right side of my body, incontinence, severe pain, a twisted spine and a noticeable limp, not to mention emotional pain and sleep deprivation.

I chose not to move forward with surgery after understanding there was only a 50% chance of recovery. I chose to begin a recovery practice of Pilates and physical therapy, as well as yoga, meditation, swimming/floating, support from amazing holistic practitioners, writing, and the development of a daily log. My recovery was enlightening and led me to teach these practices to movers with similar injury presentations. However, I always felt that I couldn't reach my last ounce of pain, my ultimate movement potential, my true healing. This is what drew me to Leah and her teachings. My body no longer continued to heal with what I was doing; I needed something new.

When I entered the room for my first class with Leah, I immediately recognized that I had been living at a level of discomfort that I had pushed away, covered up, and tucked inside. I was cued through gentle movements of the spine and awareness exercises that reminded me that I could relax. Through a mixture of prone, supine, standing, seated, and partnering exercises I began to feel parts of my spine, pelvis, and feet reawakening. I felt stability that did not require fear or bracing. I was able to move with a sense of openness and internal support. I was creating space for energetic flow and an overall positive movement experience. There were moments when I felt as if I wasn't doing much at all, but I stayed with it. I felt the "almost nothing" and realized it allowed space for a deep opening my body craved. I noticed that the exercises I learned in class prepared my body in gentle and intuitive ways. The combination of activation and release exercises communicated a wider range of movement opportunity and less pain.

Through Leah's thoughtfully researched sequence of movements I began to truly FEEL a wave of physical sensation and deep currents in my nervous system washing over me. My lower back began opening up and I could feel parts of my spine that I hadn't felt since before my injury. There was no denying the changes that were occurring.

There was another reason that I continued to heal in this class: the positive movement experience is palpable in the room and every question I had around my own pain felt valid and was answered with an "experiment" to try. I can only wish that these classes were offered everywhere, breaking the stigma around the pelvic floor.

There has been much study and research around the fascia (a layer of strong, stretchy tissue that covers, separates, or holds together different organs, muscles, blood vessels, and nerves) and how much it holds, from a natural coiling, to tension, to our stories and traumas. Some say, "the issues are in the tissues." With this in mind, I started to understand more about my own holding patterns. The exercises we did in yoga weren't changing my musculoskeletal injuries, they were re-patterning and re-orienting existing movement choices that began to change subconsciously, which in my philosophy means true change. What was revelatory for me was that this was exactly the practice that I engaged in with the dancers I taught and the Pilates students I coached. Yet, I wasn't able to get to the depth of my own healing with the knowledge I knew. This practice is unique and very special, and for me critical in getting to the ultimate part of my healing–the best part.

सत्य

What is Rooting?

"The mind rests at the place where the body touches the earth. Let the weight of the body sink into the place–for example, the feet. Intensify the weight pressing down, as if the foot would like to sink into the earth, and then feel the power of that downward movement flowing through the body. As the roots of a tree deepen and widen into the earth, so the branches above expand into the sky." *Orit Sen-Gupta*

Gentle pelvic tilts

Lengthens the spine, relieves lower back tension, strengthens the core system, connects pelvis with the feet, stabilizes legs and sacrum

Lie down on your back with the knees bent and feet parallel on the ground at hip width. Root your feet. Draw an imaginary line from the center of your heels to the sitting bones. Inhale. Exhale and intensify the rooting of the feet, the pelvis responding in a posterior tilt (as if lengthening the tail bone toward the heels and slightly up), the pelvic floor collecting itself in *isuf*. Inhale, release the pelvis until the sacrum feels stable and relax your pelvic floor. To fine-tune your practice, do not overly squeeze the glutes, keep the

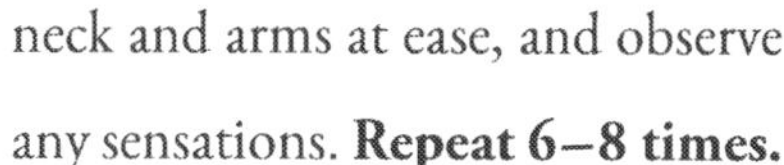
neck and arms at ease, and observe any sensations. **Repeat 6–8 times.**

Deborah

Abdominal and breast surgeries ~ Bladder control ~ Rectal surgery ~ Confidence

Multiple abdominal and breast surgeries left me with poor core strength and no rectus abdominal muscles. I had chosen a TRAM reconstruction as a repair for bilateral mastectomies. (To perform TRAM reconstruction after mastectomy, surgeons use tissue from the lower abdomen–traverse rectus abdominal muscle–to create a new breast.) I would not choose that again!

I have always had a problem with bladder leakage, even before babies. With the birth of my first child, I suffered major episiotomies affecting my rectal control. Over forty years ago I had rectal surgery after the birth of my second child. I did all kinds of physical therapy, including grasping inserts vaginally, which I was expected to do every day. I tried but I was younger and busy with babies. I am 75 now.

I needed to find something I could do on a regular basis that would make me comfortable with what was going on in my body and let me feel that I was doing all I could do to improve my pelvic floor and general fitness. Surgery is not an option. Years ago, I investigated doing mesh surgery (a procedure involving inserting a mesh sling underneath the middle part of the urethra) but realized it was out of the question. I also investigated InterStim Therapy–implanting an electronic device in the pelvic floor that produces a current creating more regular contraction and relaxation to better control urination. That option in the end didn't work well for me.

I have worn a pad for over 40 years. My physical therapist suggested toddler potty training–trying a day without wearing a pad. Psychologically and physiologically wearing a pad may inhibit my ability to control leakage. Physical therapy taught me to do Kegels correctly–bringing something up the "elevator" and down the "elevator," which helps. I still need to train my bladder not to go every hour. My mother, who passed away at 98, did not have the benefit of this training. By the time she was 85 she suffered from significant leakage.

In yoga we do not just tighten external sphincters. Learning proper breathing has helped me move with a greater degree of ease without fear of leakage. In Leah's yoga class I have learned that there are many people with pelvic problems and this has given me greater confidence. The flow and awareness between movements and activities while breathing effectively is most significant to me. The simple things in yoga are the really important ones in terms of my mental health and my ability to move on.

सत्य

Setu Bandhasana – Bridge Pose

Strengthens back, legs, and glutes; stabilizes pelvis; relaxes neck and shoulders

Lie down on your back and bend your knees, the feet parallel on the floor at hip width, the arms alongside your body, palms down. Root the feet down and lift the pelvis off the ground to a slight hover. Through several breaths continue lifting your pelvis while staying rooted in the feet and active through your thighs and glutes. Release the shoulders and the back of the head to the mat. Hold your bridge pose for several breaths; your back should not hurt. If you experience any pain, go back to the hover, and hold there. Lower your pelvis slowly down. **Repeat 3–5 times.**

Shira

Urine leakage ~ Jaw pain ~ Bulimia ~ Body image ~ Precise breathing

My pelvic floor issues began nine years ago, after giving birth to my first daughter. It took me a while to notice something was off. I clearly remember the moment when on a short hike I suddenly lost my footing and fell and had a serious leak (so bad I had to change). At the time I did not really understand what was going on, and embarrassment prevented me from seeking treatment. I dealt with it like I do with many other life discomforts—by disconnecting and ignoring. Four years later I gave birth to my second child, and a year and a half after that to my third, youngest daughter. After giving birth for the third time, ignoring was not an option anymore. Leaks were so frequent (several times a day) that I couldn't run, dance, or play with my girls without worrying. I noticed that I was avoiding physical activities I used to enjoy, including sexual contact with my husband. I started wearing thick menstruation pads to protect myself.

At that time, I heard that a physiotherapist was giving a lecture on pelvic floor health at my kibbutz, the community in Israel where I live. I began working with her and tried everything from simple exercises, biofeedback, and electricity, to extremely painful internal manipulations (pressing and massaging the internal muscles to release them). Nothing seemed to help. I couldn't really do the exercises because I couldn't make my inner muscles move or contract as I was asked to. Uncomfortable with the intrusive interventions, and disappointed by the lack of improvement, I gave up. Treatment with a different physiotherapist was better, gentler, and more holistic, but I still couldn't really participate in exercising the inner muscles. I started looking into surgery and even got a referral from my gynecologist.

After nine years of distancing myself from treating my inner muscles' weakness, I began doing yoga sessions with Leah on Skype. In our second or third session I could feel my body "listen" to me for the first time. With very gentle breathing exercises and precise images that I could visualize, I got my pelvic floor muscles to move and collect themselves. This moment was so powerful for me that my eyes filled with tears.

During the yoga sessions, I noticed that my jaw muscles were tense as I was practicing the breathing and trying to focus on pelvic floor muscles. I was instructed to focus on the vaginal lips (labia) and I could feel my mouth lips responding instead. This holistic approach enabled me to fine-tune my practice. For example, in our last session Leah corrected the use of my lips while breathing and making the sound shhh and that enabled me to better connect with my pelvic floor muscles. As she explained the connections between the mouth and pelvic floor muscles, my history of bulimia came up. I recalled that often after vomiting I had some urine leak. I had never considered this connection before. Although I have been "symptom-free" for about 20 years, the muscle connection feels so significant and vivid.

My eating disorder history affected my body image and created a hostile relationship between me and my body. I now had to reexamine my relationship with my body, because self-compassion, self-acceptance, and a nonjudgmental approach is a basic condition and foundation for the work we do.

With yoga, I have noticed a significant reduction in leak frequency, even when coughing, sneezing, and being physically active. I even switched the thick pad that I used for years to a thin daily panty liner. I feel more comfortable carrying heavy things, running, and dancing freely and spontaneously. And I feel a significant change in my experience during sex. In the past I virtually felt nothing during intercourse, and now I have more sensation and experience more pleasure as a result.

I still have a very long way to go, and practicing on my own is a huge struggle for me. I can definitely feel the difference between when I practice and when I don't. But for me the most important thing, the magic, was getting to reconnect, physically and emotionally, to the parts of me that I was distanced from and had ignored for so long.

सत्य

Shhh . . . In a table position

Stabilizes pelvis and shoulders; strengthens arms, wrists, and core system; uses sound to accentuate activation of pelvic floor

Come to a table position, align your shoulders above your wrists and your hips above your knees. Spread your fingers, and root the hands, shins, and tops of the feet down. Take a full round of breath to elongate the spine. Inhale and relax the belly. Exhale, make the sound *shhh* . . . (as if calming a baby) and contract the navel toward the spine along with *isuf*. Inhale, relax the belly, mouth, and pelvic floor muscles completely. **Repeat 3–5 times.**

Mark (told by Leah)

Pelvic floor dysfunction ~ Hypertense pelvic floor muscles ~ Injuries ~ Body awareness

Mark is a tall, athletic guy in his 30s. He works as a strength and conditioning coach, and he knows his body. Mark contacted me because he was frustrated. When working out he noticed that his muscles weren't working together properly, and he felt limited and restrained by the lack of function in his pelvic floor. When we first met, he told me, "I feel like there is nothing there . . . like it's just empty. Nothing." While many women I work with suffer from tremendous pain and describe their pelvic floor feeling as if on fire, I now found myself working with a man who asked for help "firing up" his pelvic floor. This was interesting, because though we were both aware that muscular tension was preventing him from feeling his pelvic floor—which often shows up in the body as lack of flexibility—this guy could do a full split on both sides! He tried different modalities of relief from the sports world and was often prescribed muscle relaxers, but this frustrated him because he wasn't looking for a quick fix. While massage therapy did temporarily relieve the inhibiting tension, this too he told me "would not stick."

Mark was aware of how the accumulation of stress and past football injuries had impacted his body, and he came for private lessons because he wanted someone to **see** *him, to see his full alignment and way of movement. In this one-on-one setting he was able to awaken internal sensation and find movement that was much more subtle and delicate than he was used to, and it worked like magic. The* *awareness of breath and focused practice of relaxation* ***before*** *moving into* ***isuf,*** *along with the work of coordinating the inner thighs and abdomen to function in unison with the pelvic floor, made a difference. From week to week, he felt better and better, stronger in his workouts of weightlifting, squat jumping, and running, and even simply walking. For the first few weeks when I would ask how he was doing he would smile and say, "I don't know what we are doing, but it works." Slowly he realized that being able to identify his own patterns of tension, and then get those muscles to gently relax, was the key: "It all comes down to body awareness and breathing," he shared. One of the exercises that made everything click for Mark was the quadruped (as he calls it coming from the sports world; I call it table or all fours) with the knees hovering above the floor. When done correctly, this exercise allows feeling the activation of the lower abdomen and the pelvic floor working in sync. It was one big* ***aha!*** *moment for Mark on his way to realizing his movement potential.*

सत्य

Hovering table

Intensifies the previous hands and knees exercise; stabilizes pelvis and shoulders; strengthens the back, arms, wrists, and entire core system

Come to a table position, align your shoulders above your wrists and your hips above your knees. Curl your toes under and implement the pebble–pearl connection (see Exercises for Training the Pelvic Floor). Breathing naturally, root into the ground with the balls of your feet and all ten fingertips, hovering the knees off the floor. Hold for several breaths or set a timer for 30 seconds. Rest. **Repeat 2–3 times.**

Yaara (told by Leah)

Pelvic floor tension ~ Pain during intercourse ~ Colitis ~ Urine leakage ~ Playfulness

I have a dear friend whose brain I've picked for years about everything pelvic floor-related. She shared my enthusiasm about the topic, came to my workshops, brainstormed on what worked and what didn't, and always encouraged me to keep up with my research and to write this book. She too is a yoga teacher, but also had experienced working with both a pelvic floor physical therapist as well as with an osteopath (a doctor who uses non-invasive treatment based on manipulation of the musculoskeletal framework). What brought her initially to these therapies was the surprising realization that she had muscle tightness. In some circles, women experiment with what is called a yoni egg (an egg-shaped crystal inserted into the vagina). When Yaara tried using the egg, she discovered that while she was able to keep the egg inside (many women with lack of muscle tone are not able to do so), she was not able to "lay the egg." She felt that something inside was overly contracted and was unable to release enough for the egg to slide out. The physical therapist she went to helped relieve some of the tension using internal massage, and also clarified something very important for Yaara, "She told me that intercourse should be pain free. I didn't know that! I had assumed my entire adult life that it was normal to experience some degree of pain during intercourse." I was astounded when Yaara shared this with me. "You thought that intercourse is ***supposed*** *to be painful?" I asked. Again, she made me recognize how valuable education on this matter is, as is having open conversations.*

After giving birth, two things prompted her growing need to figure out how to work with her pelvic floor muscles. Urine leakage was one of them, as well as a very bad attack of colitis (inflammatory bowel disease). Yaara lost a lot of weight and spent hours in the bathroom, some days with severe diarrhea 20 times a day. Her pelvic floor and specifically the sphincters were weakened by the birth, and she also suffered with urinary incontinence and the inability to feel her body in the way she wanted. She had to retrain the muscles. What I enjoyed so thoroughly in the process of sharing as a friend in her journey was how open and delighted she became with each new discovery. She kept a playful approach, asked questions, and reflected out loud. She built up her strength, and at the same time learned to recognize when she was overly tensing her internal muscles. After a workshop she shared, "I learned that the collecting of the pelvic floor muscles can be very delicate. The instruction to just look at the very subtle, delicate movement at the ***beginning*** *of the contraction still moves me and enables me to access a formerly inaccessible part of my body."*

सत्य

Adho Mukha Svanasana– Downward Facing Dog

Strengthens shoulders, wrists, and arms; stretches hamstrings, calves, and pelvic floor; relaxes neck and ankles

Come to a table position; align your shoulders above your wrists and your hips above your knees. Spread your fingers wide, keep your arms straight and curl your toes under. Press your hands into the floor as if pushing it away. Root the balls of your feet down and lift your hips up; your legs will begin to straighten. Lengthen the heels toward the ground (though they do not have to touch, and your knees can stay bent), elongate your spine and relax your neck. To fine-tune your posture, observe how the pelvic floor stretches gently as it also responds in *isuf* to the rooting down of hands and feet. Hold for several deep breaths or **set the timer for 1 minute, building up to 2–3 minutes.**

Shalabasana – Locust Pose

Strengthens back, glutes, hamstrings, entire core system

Lie down on your belly with the legs long and parallel, the arms by your sides, palms down. Place your chin or forehead on the ground. Press the tops of your feet into the floor and activate your legs. Engage your core by lifting the pubic bone up toward the navel and creating a sense of *isuf*. Lift your chest, legs, and arms off the ground; keep the neck long. Imagine squeezing a ball lightly between your inner thighs. To fine-tune your posture, reach out from all edges of your body while remaining deeply connected at the belly. The lips and jaw are soft. Hold for several breaths. Rest. **Repeat 3–5 times.**

Claire

Childhood sexual trauma ~ Childbirth as an emotional trigger ~ Slowing down and paying attention ~ Courage

> *My body was mine as I danced and moved, one moment at a time. It was a world all my own, a world no one could touch, disturb, invade, harm. . . Only concentrating on my breath, my pulse, the beauty of the movement . . . I was my own feeling.*

I never thought I would be able to have children. I can't remember how old I was when my mother caught me masturbating, exploring my body, trying to figure things out. I do however, remember her shocked, shaming reaction and words to me, "Sweet girls don't do that! You will hurt yourself and maybe never be able to have a baby!" And I thought, Dear God, if just touching myself will do that, then I'm already ruined because what they've done to me is much worse.

I was a little girl. I had curls and played with dolls, climbed trees, adored dancing, and lived in terror that the molestation I experienced night after night for more than five years would never stop. That I was broken forever. I became an expert at holding my breath, pretending I was a statue, not moving or talking, and most importantly, not feeling anything. Dying a little each time. Trauma, fear, disorder, stress, shock–there are really no adequate words for what went on for far too long.

Years later, I was elated to be carrying another soul in my belly. "You're pregnant!"

was one of the happiest things I had ever heard. I practiced many breathing techniques to relax and center my mind, and I learned about my pelvis and the muscles that would be key in delivering my baby. But truthfully, nothing had prepared me for what was coming. For years something in me felt proud that though I was secretly damaged it didn't keep me from having loving relationships and a healthy sex life. But see, what I had never heard about was that sensations and feelings during labor and childbirth can trigger feelings from sexual abuse and trauma. My healthy, educated adult mind—which till that point had been playing its part in saving me from going through any more pain associated with what I had experienced as a child, and that for all those years had worked so hard to spare me from any record of that past trauma—dropped its shield when I was in labor. The physical pain of childbirth, an arduous 31-hour labor of my son, and the overwhelming lack of control over what my body was going through, brought back unexpected and unbearable past pain. I did not want to feel it. Even though the payoff was a baby. Thankfully, I was able to have a vaginal delivery, but only aided by an epidural. I realized then that the disconnect with my pelvis, cervix, and vagina, and all the attached emotions was vast, even at nearly 30 years old. Childbirth had reopened old wounds. I would begin a new journey of self-discovery. Because of my dedication, three years later I delivered a baby girl in six hours. A water birth with no medication. I was ready this time. I felt connected to all women. I call this a victory!

Through trusted friendships, counseling, exercise, and regular yoga practice, I made great strides to overcome my fears and pain. I learned that my mind, breath, heart, tissues, and bones are connected by a strong, rooted, and loving cord that feels every emotion together—sometimes laughter, often tears—all healing and all valid in our body's work to strengthen and grow.

Though I have practiced yoga throughout my adult life, practicing yoga with a particular focus on the pelvic floor, I believe has helped me the most. Till then I was working from every part of my body except the pelvis. I loved big movements; I loved backbends and poses where I felt an opening of my heart to be bold and give myself as a strong and fearless presence to the world I love so much. The pelvis was the dark closet that I did not want to open, or even let air and breath into. But when I was finally unafraid to make peace with the area of my body that was such a source of pain, a space opened up for grief and release. When at the end of class, I lay still and focused on my body's response, I remembered many silent tears dripping down my face. Yoga brought me into a more acute awareness of my body by doing the very challenging work of slowing down and paying attention to this place that I was once ashamed of, but that now I feel as a source of comfort and strength. I am still learning and want to continue healing and strengthening myself, no matter how difficult at times.

And my journey will continue, as does everyone's.

सत्य

Bhujangasana– Cobra Pose

Stretches the back and abdominals, strengthens the arms and legs, opens the chest

Lie down on your belly with your legs long, press the tops of your feet into the ground, and activate your legs. Plant your hands in front of you at shoulder-width apart, palms down, and place your forehead on the ground. Root your hands down, lift your chest off the floor as your arms begin to straighten (keep the elbows as bent as needed, the back should not hurt). Press your inner thighs into the midline; this activation echoes upward in *isuf.* To fine-tune your posture, soften your face, slide your shoulder blades down, and lengthen your neck. Hold for several deep breaths. Rest. **Repeat 1–3 times.**

Scott (told by Leah)

Severe injury ~ Stiffness and tightness ~ Irregularity ~ The pebble

A number of years ago, Scott, who suffers from REM sleeping disorder (in which the paralysis that normally occurs during REM sleep is only partial), sleepwalked onto his spiral staircase on the second floor of his house and went tumbling down. He broke his back in four places (he now has a metal rod through his spine), 18 ribs, and his left scapula, and hit his head so hard he almost bled to death on the floor where his wife found him. He spent four weeks in a trauma hospital with traumatic brain and spinal cord injury. During that period, he recalls being extremely angry, terribly harsh and mean to anyone who came close, deeply frustrated as he was barely able to walk, and disoriented. After his transfer to a rehabilitation hospital, he began to improve and his memory slowly returned. He was told that it would take a few months to recover and that he would be leaving in a wheelchair, but after six weeks thanks to the wonderful care he received and his determination, Scott was able to walk out of the hospital.

A common effect of injury is how protectively tight the muscles around the hurt area can become. In Scott's case the pelvis became extremely tight, and the side effect of this, and the reason for which he was referred for pelvic floor physical therapy, manifested itself in difficulty emptying his bowels. Unable to relax the pelvic floor muscles, Scott describes his system as feeling blocked, as if there was an internal injury with a persistent dull ache anytime he needed to use the bathroom. When Scott shares his PT experience, he becomes very uncomfortable. Though the physical therapist was wonderful and down to earth he says, having her finger inserted through the anus to internally massage the scar tissue "was painful and humiliating." Scott was relieved to be referred to yoga.

I met an open-minded man who, though taken aback by his own vulnerability, worked hard to focus and follow instructions. To his surprise, he discovered how weak his inner thighs were. He did not expect simple exercises to be so challenging and to be sorer from a gentle yoga session than from working out at the gym with a personal trainer. "I should be strong enough to do this," he would say, perplexed. But these were muscles that Scott was not used to using. And it isn't just Scott. I see many students with strong quadriceps, rectus abdominis, and back muscles. But the body isn't working in coordination, and the pelvic floor . . . well it is just left out!

To help Scott, we focused on two main things: stretching (mainly the inner thighs, back, and hamstrings); and guiding him to locate the imaginary pebble, lift it up by controlling his contraction and building internal strength, and release it by relaxing the pelvic floor, mainly the anal sphincter. When I interviewed Scott for this book he admitted with a sigh, "I hate that damn pebble. I never thought I could do it. I thought this is crazy as hell. Something guys don't do." Yet he shared that once he really focused on coordinating his breath with the movement, "It was not the pebble but the thought process of what you are trying to make that pebble do that makes those muscles move. It's crazy, but it works." While in the beginning his muscles wouldn't respond, he now describes a deep internal lifting sensation that ends with a turn inwards and up that I never mentioned. This is him ***experiencing his own body.*** *Scott has learned to release tense muscles, and to calm and steady his breath. He enjoys the stretching tremendously, something he never thought he would. He has gained awareness of his body, externally and internally, and no longer dreads going to the bathroom.*

सत्य

Leg stretches

Stretches hamstrings, stabilizes pelvis, elongates the back

Lie down on your back, lift your right leg up and wrap a strap (or belt) around the ball of your foot. Extend your left leg out on the floor (if this is challenging, bend your left knee and place your foot on the ground). Extend the right foot up towards the ceiling. Anchor your pelvis evenly on the floor, keep your shoulders down on the mat and your elbows close to your body. Inhale and elongate the leg; exhale, soften your hip joint and pull your leg gently closer to your body. Focus on your deep breathing. **Hold this posture for 1–2 minutes before switching legs.**

Mary

Prolapsed uterus ~ Retired veteran ~ Grief over the past ~ Embracing change

I was in my battle dress uniform—camouflage and combat boots—when I walked into the examination room at the Army base hospital for a typical annual physical and pap smear. I was in stirrups when the OBGYN conducting the exam stated rather matter-of-factly, "You have a prolapsed uterus." I did not ask any questions and the female doctor did not elaborate. That is the first memory I have concerning a prolapse. For the briefest moment, as I walked back to the barracks after the exam, I wondered what it meant to have a prolapse. But just as quickly as I wondered about it, it fled my thoughts. At 23, there were more important things on my mind such as what outfit I was going to wear to the club that Saturday. That was over 30 years ago. I was 17 years old when I joined the military in 1984.

The rigors of a physically demanding military career affect every individual differently, but it will affect everyone. When I began my career, I gave no thought to the impact it would play on my body in the long term. There is no "easier" or "less rigorous" job to be had in the military—especially a military at war. I was in my mid-forties when I spoke to a fellow servicemember who told me that she had a hysterectomy because her uterus protruded from her vaginal opening. I made a frantic beeline to my gynecologist's office and requested to see her immediately. "I need to see you because I have a prolapse!" I said, as if I had just been notified moments earlier. Of course my doctor looked at me as if this is no revelation to her and should not be for me either. "Yes, you do," she said. "Well, I had no idea what that means," I explained.

When I returned from my deployment to Afghanistan, I was diagnosed with an anterior prolapse—a cystocele. I had sought out a specialist and was also diagnosed, to no one's surprise, with urinary stress incontinence. I was a broken spirit. My doctor told me that was one of the reasons she recommended a hysterectomy and explained that I stood a higher chance of having a protrusion. She went on to say that the only thing holding my uterus in place was multiple fibroids. I felt hopeless.

A retired veteran at 52, I moved back home and decided to join a local gym. After an initial assessment with a representative, it was determined that I should postpone joining the fitness center and seek medical attention for my organ prolapse. I was requested to consult with a physical therapist. I remember my eyes welling up with tears with the knowledge that physical therapy was available. Never once had I considered physical therapy for my issues—I never knew that there was a non-invasive option. As I sat in the office crying, it wasn't because I was advised to cease exercise until further notice, but rather because, for the first time, I was given hope beyond surgery. It took a full twelve months of wrangling with insurance providers before I finally received a referral. The day I walked into the physical therapist's office, I felt a weight lifting off my shoulders and I shed many tears. At my initial meeting I saw a postcard displayed on the counter advertising yoga for women with pelvic floor issues.

I took a workshop with Leah called Pelvic Health and Deep Core Strength, and it taught how we women could strengthen our abdominals in relation to pelvic floor strength and stability. But for me it was far more transformative emotionally and mentally, and had a profound impact. It provided an intimate, safe space to sit in a circle of women and open our hearts and minds to an in-depth healing process. We shared our thoughts and struggles, and the effect on our lives. We were given a forum to give up some of our grief, as much as we wanted to let go of.

I had participated in yoga classes before, but the pelvic health classes were different. These types of medical issues are not widely talked about, and until then, I had felt like I was suffering alone. In this specialized class I was granted a private space among others with similar issues to grow and learn through the processes. It let me embrace me, and helped me heal more deeply. I realized that being fully present is being totally tuned in to, and aware of, my body. I gained the ability to recognize and feel—actually feel—my pelvic floor and make it a positive part of my body. It had been a failing part and, therefore, a shunned, ashamed part of me for so long that I had to get reacquainted with it. I had to embrace it and learn to work with it again.

In the military, training comes in phases. Phase Zero is often referred to as the crawl stage, and then you pick up the pace in the walk phase. By the time you reach the run phase of training, you should be relying very heavily on muscle memory. The five months of physical therapy were the beginning of me changing my thoughts about my body - learning about muscle groups working in sync and allowing myself to embrace positivity. Physical therapy laid the foundation, and yoga the building blocks. I found myself transitioning into the run stage—what a great feeling!

I am taking necessary precautions now and have embraced my limitations; I no longer pick up items that are too heavy. In the military, I wore a thirty-plus-pound backpack, along with other equipment that added weight. No one tells us this can have a profound effect. We would march fifteen or more miles and sometimes run with this equipment. While this may not seem like a big deal, it was impacting my life and wearing my body down. If I had known, I could have taken steps to preserve my pelvic floor from the moment I found out I had a prolapse.

I was the woman whose gynecologist recommended a hysterectomy. I was the woman who was fitted for a pessary and recommended for surgery. Today I am the woman who has not had a hysterectomy nor surgery. I am far healthier emotionally and physically due in no small measure to the pelvic floor training my yoga teacher provides, and for that I will be forever grateful. They say people come in your life for a season and a reason—this was a necessary season, one filled with sunshine.

सत्य

Figure 4 stretch

Stretches inner and outer thighs and buttocks, stabilizes pelvis, relaxes the back

Lie down on your back and bend your knees, feet on the ground. Place your right ankle just above your left knee. Flex your right foot. Lift the legs, thread the right arm in between the legs, and clasp your hands on the back of your left thigh. Hug your legs towards your chest. Relax your shoulders, mouth, and forehead, and breath slowly and deeply. **Hold this posture for 1–2 minutes before switching legs.**

Liz (told by Leah)

Traumatic birth ~ Painful periods ~ Hysterectomy ~ Numbness ~ Trauma ~ Emotional release ~ Pleasure

Liz starts our interview with the story of giving birth to her daughter, who she calls her miracle baby, twelve years earlier. Towards the end of her pregnancy, she felt something was very wrong. Ignoring her doula's advice to rest and walk it off, she went to the emergency room and was rushed into an emergency C-section. Her daughter, born with a rare complication, was then rushed into a difficult abdominal surgery. The emotional impact of a traumatic birth, along with having a newborn who needed (and still needs) round-the-clock care, did not allow Liz to recover properly from her C-section. She was hospitalized alongside her infant with severely infected surgical wounds.

When she talks about that time, she says it feels like someone else's story. Liz is one of the most positive, smiley people I know. She is focused on the miracle of her daughter's survival and how lucky she is to be her mother. When I ask about what brought her to my class, she tells me about the hysterectomy she had several months before we met. For a very long time Liz refused to contemplate having this surgery. Attached to what the reproductive system symbolizes with regard to identity, many female students of mine have shared their struggle in making this decision. For Liz it was life changing. For years she had suffered long (seven to ten days), heavy, and painful periods, and since giving birth she had bleeding in between them as well. Intercourse was painful, but even after intercourse she would have painful uterine and abdominal cramping. When she got to a place where she could barely function, anemic and fatigued, with all the energy she could afford geared toward caregiving, she agreed to a hysterectomy. Though the many doctors she had seen over the years failed to diagnose her, now in surgery the operating doctors found endometriosis (an abnormal growth of tissue outside the uterus causing pelvic pain), polyps (growths attached to the inner wall of the uterus), fibroids (benign tumors growing in the womb and known for causing abdominal pain and heavy periods), and stage 1 uterine cancer. So once more, Liz who had just undergone major surgery, experienced tremendous levels of stress because of the cancer diagnosis, but could not find a moment for self-care and recovery. Thankfully, she managed to recover fully over time. But although the incisions were abdominal, she describes feeling left with a bizarre sort of numbness, especially in the vagina. "During intercourse I felt like it was an out-of-body experience. Total disconnect."

Before having her child, Liz loved yoga. So when she came across my pelvic health-focused class through a colleague of mine who was helping her manage her TMJ (temporomandibular joint dysfunction–pain in the jaw and surrounding muscles), she was excited to try it. One of the things that often comes up in my classes is how many women also suffer from TMJ or tension around the jaw. Liz has been suffering from this condition for over twenty years, triggering ongoing migraines. Our conversation took place in her living room on a beautiful Friday afternoon and was lighthearted and filled with laughter. As we talked, so many details that did not seem connected in Liz's mind, began painting a fuller picture for both of us, for instance the realization of how distinctly the jaw connects with the pelvic floor.

Liz shared an unexpected release that she had experienced during yoga a few weeks earlier: "Side plank was so intense I was shaking, and suddenly I started crying. To me it felt like my abdominals releasing emotional sadness. So much trauma in my reproductive system and abdominals. . . ."

We allow the body to experience and release what it needs to. This is the nature of somatic healing. Liz describes how ever since she started taking class, sensation is returning, sex is pleasurable, and she feels more control over her body. Liz shares that she never noticed before how much the pelvic floor muscles are involved and engage in all the things she does throughout the day. She describes how much yoga has helped with her alignment and managing her stress, and how working with isuf has brought back the most intimate connection not just to her own body but to her husband as well. I love it when Liz describes how the instructions I give in class for being physically aware of something, makes her feel her body, and that in order to really feel, she has to be mentally tuned in. "It is all interlocked," she says with a smile of amazement.

We almost finish our interview when Liz acknowledges with a sigh that she feels there is so much more in her history that is related to our conversation. After we have been chatting for over an hour I feel comfortable asking if she has experienced any sexual trauma. I can see the split second of understanding on her face. Yes, she says, sexual trauma is a part of her past. Liz describes her young self as the typical latchkey kid. Her parents were divorced and busy with career and social life. Liz tells me "I sought comfort and affection from whoever would give it. It started as early as kindergarten." By the time she reached fifth grade she had experienced six incidents in which she found herself a part of situations she didn't feel comfortable with, including oral sex. At eleven she lost her virginity. Through her teens she remembers acting out—drinking, smoking pot, having sex with many men who did not treat her well, and as a result being sent to "bad kids camp." I can feel Liz's grief when she says that her mother never made time for her, never talked to her, and that what she learned about sex and intimacy was through television and sneaking pornography. By the time she was seventeen and met the man who she would later marry she describes feeling dirty. "I was so messed up in my thinking, so ashamed. He was respectful, but I had so much pain by then, so much trauma." When I ask Liz if she thinks there may be a connection between feeling that way, feeling dirty, to then beginning to have extremely heavy, painful periods, she just says, "Wow."

What was so moving to me and clear through Liz's story is how layered all of our stories are. How at the end of the day we can't really separate what we feel in our relationships and the histories we carry, from the way we think about and experience our bodies. Though one thing links to the other, the beauty in the practice is that we work hard at coming onto the yoga mat clean of our own judgment and labels. Whether it's stretching the hamstring or doing a plank, our mental focus is on executing something physical, and that in turn allows for the emotional to surface and release. At a moment like this I wish I could attach Liz's recorded voice when she says how wonderful she has been feeling since starting to practice yoga, stretching out the word a m a z i n g in a singing voice. She makes me laugh out loud when she ends our interview with, "I have so many issues, but thankfully I can pee and poop just fine."

सत्य

Happy baby

Stretches the back, hips, legs, and pelvic floor

Lie down on your back with your knees bent to the chest. Grab the outer part of your feet or your big toes. If this is challenging hold behind your knees. Allow the legs to fall wide open. Your pelvic floor is relaxed and stretched. Relax your shoulders toward the floor, relax your buttocks and your thighs.

Hold for several long breaths.

Pelvic-Feet Connection

"There are moments where I realize that all I need to do is just plant my feet more firmly into the ground. I'm not trying to hold myself upright from just my pelvic floor anymore." Sandra shared this with me one day after class. It seems evident intellectually that the very foundation on which we stand is important, but understanding the role of the feet from within the body is powerful. The feet are these incredible, ingeniously engineered structures, with 26 bones, 31 joints, and 20 intrinsic muscles. Awakening the feet so that they are dynamic and healthy is reflected in our balance, and the position of our knees, hips, and pelvis. Utilizing the focus on the feet and the action of rooting the center of the heel, ball of the big toe, and ball of the pinky is extremely beneficial in feeling the pelvic floor as responsive and vibrant. When we gently press the feet downward–as if that downward movement can be infinite–something will flow back up through the body and through the base of the pelvis as well. That pulsing responsive relationship between the feet and pelvic floor is something we cultivate very clearly in standing yoga postures. But it can be practiced every time you sit and stand up. Observe that as you shift your weight to or from your feet, the pelvic floor engages gently as well. While Sandra's tendency was to keep her body straight by forcefully contracting her internal muscles, many others stand upright with no internal energy activated at all. Pay attention throughout your day while in different positions, walking, and transitioning from one position to another, to how the feet and pelvic floor relate to one another.

Sandra

Chronic hip, lower abdominal, and pelvic pain ~ Body awareness ~ Self-worth

Yoga with Leah had been recommended to me for several years, but I had already lost trust in the fitness world. In every endeavor to get strong and recover from the hip surgery that I had at twenty-nine, I felt like those who tried to help me never really "saw" me, and each time I ended up worse than when I began. People around me, including medical professionals, couldn't accept or believe the pain I felt, or my inability to bounce back post-surgery. I suffered constant pain in my pelvis, lower back, and hip flexors, and stabbing pain in my lower abdomen. Then, somehow, I met my pelvic floor physical therapist, a woman who has made her life's work exploring women's "hoo-ha's," and God bless her for it! In my mid-thirties I was validated for the first time that my pain was real. When my PT examined my pelvic floor's resting tone, on a scale of zero to ten, it was nine. Even she was astonished by the constant contracted state my pelvic floor muscles were in.

My past toxic relationships kept me on a path of continually trying to prove myself to others in order to feel worthy, strong, beautiful, and ultimately accepted and loved. I was repeatedly objectified and ridiculed by an emotionally and sexually abusive boyfriend. When we broke up, the hurtful words still lingered. My need to prove myself worthy led me to obsessively train for sprint (mini) triathlons. I was quickly aware that I did not enjoy these competitive experiences that felt damaging to my body, but in my broken spirit, to "quit" would be to fail, proving all the insults to be true. My pressing on just left me defeated and empty. And the hip surgery left me with years of chronic pain. Now in my early thirties, I had another reason I wanted to heal—a wonderful man, my soon-to-be husband. And yet, I feared what I should be celebrating—sex! Thoughts of intercourse brought anxiety. I knew in my heart that I needed to learn the mind-body connection. It was the key to opening up the door to my recovery.

In the pelvic health class, the things that I used to be complimented for in other yoga classes, postures that looked impressive externally but didn't feel good from the inside, Leah would correct, and encourage me to "do less." This class, truly, became the crux of my healing. I felt that she could see deep inside me, and I almost felt that maybe she could feel what I could feel. In yoga, I found the comfort I needed in order to be honest with myself in exploring my strengths and weaknesses. I learned how to calm the busy wavelengths of my extreme self-awareness. And I learned how the threads that bind me and cause my pain can also be the threads to unwind me. Yoga has given me the power to create communication pathways within myself to help with self-soothing and ease when I feel tension and pain arising.

After about a year in the pelvic class Leah encouraged me to join her regular Vijnana Yoga class. I was very anxious about attempting something new as I was afraid of falling back into old habits and creating tension where I had just learned to release it. But with the knowledge and growth I gained, I slowly opened myself up to a beautiful new practice. This new class has been what has changed my whole self-perception and self-appreciation.

My journey in yoga has led to healing of many sorts. I now know that I'm the one who needs to love me most and, it's not about proving myself to others. My relationship with and faith in God tells me that I am wonderfully made. Yoga is my physical manifestation that helps me even when I don't feel strong to know that I can endure, and that I am beautiful no matter my size, shape, or strength. When I "am yoga" I am the real Me. And I am becoming a Me I love.

सत्य

Tadasana– Mountain Pose

Attention to feet and alignment of the whole body

Stand up with your feet parallel and close together. Extend your arms alongside your body, and relax your shoulders, your fingers long and soft. Ground the center of your heels and the balls of your feet–the ball of the big toe as well as the pinky. Observe the natural arches of your feet and how the toes touch the ground. Root your feet down and engage the top of your inner thighs.

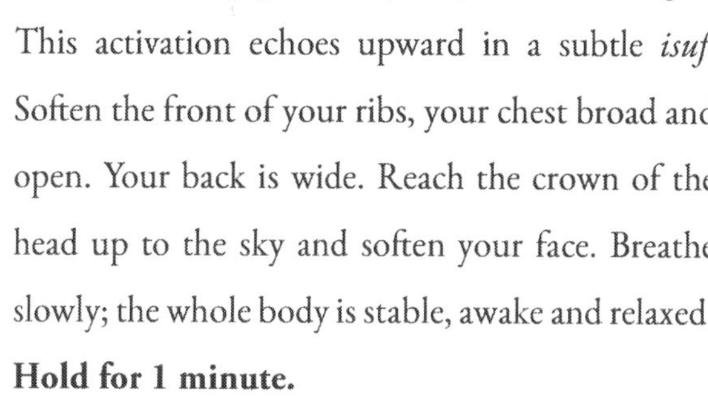

This activation echoes upward in a subtle *isuf.* Soften the front of your ribs, your chest broad and open. Your back is wide. Reach the crown of the head up to the sky and soften your face. Breathe slowly; the whole body is stable, awake and relaxed. **Hold for 1 minute.**

Roger (told by Leah)

Prostate problems ~ Quality of life

Roger passed away recently. I worked with him for several years for a one-hour session each week. When it came to sharing his private experiences, he was a man of few words. Roger was referred to me by his wife. He acknowledged how stiff his body felt—which did not help with playing golf. Improved golfing was our main objective. We spent a lot of time in chair pose, coordinating movement of eyes, neck, and bounce from the feet, pretending to swing our golf club. He also spoke in passing about the effects of prostate cancer that he had recovered from several years earlier, mainly the occasional leakage of urine. In his late seventies, he did everything he could to take good care of himself. I admired that about him. He reminded me of my father whom I had lost about a year before Roger passed, and who I had wished would care for himself a little more like Roger did. My father struggled with his prostate and he frequently went to the restroom. I remember him telling me once that the pelvic floor health education I give is wonderful, but that I don't understand prostates and that nothing could help with that. He was my father, and it is a sensitive topic, so I silently disagreed. Roger and I, however, worked on pelvic health without really talking about it; engaging the core in conjunction with slow, deep breaths, and the pelvic floor muscles (I could say to imagine he is stopping the flow of urine, and that was okay.) I cherished our time together, how he loved life, and how he strived for better health always. From his family I know that he thought of yoga as improving his overall quality of life. Although most people associate pelvic floor concerns with women, many men aged 50 and up struggle with fully emptying their bladder, discomfort, urgency, and leakage. This is real, and this is also life. I will miss Roger very much. And I miss my father, with whom I wish I had had the courage to talk more openly about how pelvic floor training can also help men.

Utkatasana– Chair Pose

Strengthens feet, legs, back, abdominals, and pelvic floor

Stand tall in mountain pose and bring your hands together in prayer position, palms touching in front of your chest. Bend your knees and send your hips back as if you were going to sit on a tall stool. Draw an imaginary line from your sitting bones to the center of your heels. Do not tuck your tailbone under. Soften your hip joints, knees, and ankles, and root your feet powerfully down. Imagine squeezing a small ball between your inner thighs; this activation echoes upward in *isuf.* Keep your arms as they are, or extend them straight over the head. To fine-tune your practice, observe how your deep core muscles are connected, and how your body, even though working with effort, is expanding and at ease. Relax your jaw. **Hold for several long breaths or set the timer to 30 seconds, building gradually to 1 minute.**

Jenny

Dyspareunia ~ Shame ~ Hypertense pelvic floor muscles ~ Relaxation with breath ~ Acceptance

I was forty-five years old when I walked into my first pelvic health yoga class. I knew I had a problem at nineteen when I experienced extreme pain with intercourse, and I sought medical help when I was twenty-six. After the first night of yoga, I got into my car and cried. I cried out of relief that there were other women who had similar problems. I cried out of sadness that I could not get medical professionals to listen to me before. I cried because I had truly believed that I was the only woman in the world to suffer what was wrong with me. And I cried because for twenty years I did not know what I had because I had never received a diagnosis.

Doctors told me there was nothing wrong with me and that I was probably just having a psychosomatic reaction–in other words, my pain was all in my head. When I described burning pain as if my tissue was on fire like an open wound, they told me I was crazy. I never mentioned the words pelvic floor because I didn't know those words. The pelvic health class started a chain reaction that brought me hope, released my shame, and alleviated some of my pain.

The breathing exercises were extremely beneficial–now I know I can do them whenever I need to, even while standing, sitting, or lying down in bed trying to relax before sleep. I suffer from hypertense pelvic floor muscles and I have learned to feel when it is at its worst and to practice my breathing to relax where I hold tension. I practice my yoga as often as possible to try to keep my symptoms to a minimum.

It took me weeks to speak to some of the other women in the class because, again, I was still telling myself that they probably didn't have the same problem that I had. But after hearing them talk to each other week after week, I finally got up the courage to talk to them. They had all gone to physical therapy for pelvic floor issues and I asked them how they got a referral. After a year of practicing yoga in this specific class, I finally got up the nerve to ask for a referral from my doctor and I began ten long months of physical therapy. After that, I started seeing a sex therapist recommended by Leah and my PT.

Today, I practice my yoga and physical therapy to maintain the progress I have made. I will probably never be able to have intercourse because too many years have gone by. Now my emotional responses have paired with my physical responses and it is hard to separate them and get my body to relax during sex. However, I cannot stress enough the progress that has been made from the shame being lifted off my shoulders. I finally told my mom and even my best friend what I had been suffering with all these years. Now, I even occasionally tell someone in a matter-of-fact way, "I have pelvic pain." I just went to my annual gynecology appointment and it was the first time in twenty years that I haven't cried from shame before the exam even started. I can also get through a pelvic exam relatively easily! That is huge for me. I just do my yoga breathing and it's virtually painless. Before I went to the pelvic health yoga class I had stopped making eye contact with my husband because my inadequacies were always on my mind. I really don't think about it much anymore.

I still occasionally have some anger that I was dismissed all these years and that I have been robbed of a "normal" marriage, although my sex therapist would scold me and tell me that a lot of people don't have a "normal" sex life. And then she would ask me what "normal" even means. I have embraced the happiness that I do have, and am grateful for contributions that I do bring to my marriage. I don't walk around all the time terrified that people are going to find out about my problem. Before I found Leah's yoga class, my pelvic floor dysfunction was always the main part of my identity even though I didn't have a name for it. Now it's just no big deal. It makes for a much happier life!

सत्य

Vajrasana– Thunderbolt Pose

Strengthens and stretches feet and legs, allows for lengthening of the spine

This next posture is challenging for many. You can modify it by sitting on a folded blanket, placed between your calves and buttocks. If the tops of your feet hurt, place a pair of rolled socks under your ankles (Jenny uses two blocks that she places between her heels and sits on). Come to sit on your heels, or modify as needed. Root the tops of your feet down and press the heels slightly inwards. Your thighs become active. Lengthen your spine, reach the top of the head up, and relax your back. Place your hands in your lap. Hold for several long breaths as you practice the subtle art of collecting and lifting the pelvic floor muscles in *isuf* and its release. Observe the shift in effort and sensation as you inhale and exhale. To fine-tune your posture, play with different sounds such as *"shh . . ."* or *"ss. . ."* and observe their effect.

Hold for 1–2 minutes.

Amelia

Chronic pelvic pain ~ Hysterectomy ~ Effects of medication ~ Self-care

I turned to yoga at a time when I was in extreme pain. My physical therapist referred me to a specialized yoga class for pelvic floor health, after I was told by doctors that as my pelvic pain was chronic, I needed to learn to live with it. Before I met my PT, local physicians recommended heavy-duty painkillers to deal with my complaints, but those didn't even dim the pain, and gave me a stomach ulcer. At its worst, it was excruciating to sit in a chair, go for a walk, or even do the simple things of daily life at home and work. My balance was off, and I would often trip and fall. I could not urinate easily. I devoted an enormous amount of time and energy reading up on what was happening with my body. My family was beside themselves with worry and I was in so much pain that I thought I would have to resign or take medical leave from my job as a writer because I could not concentrate. The medical cocktail I was taking, and my extreme fatigue and pain levels, made it virtually impossible to think. It got to the point where I sought out the help of a specialist five-hundred miles away, who shortly after my 38th birthday diagnosed me with pelvic floor dysfunction and chronically hypertense muscles, and prescribed pelvic floor physical therapy. Although the physical therapy was so painful that I had to take the afternoon off after a session to go home to lie down, it helped. My PT promised she would get me through my flare-up, and she did! She then recommended adding a yoga practice for breathing support, flexibility, and education on how to relax my pelvic floor muscles. After a few months of PT and the specialized yoga class, and once I had the major pain flare-up under control, I even added Leah's regular Vijnana yoga classes to my schedule. Both yoga classes together helped me establish a home routine in the mornings and evenings—a lifeline in a dark time.

Somehow, in the midst of my darker foggy days, when my mental clarity felt like it was on vacation, I was a hot mess emotionally, and the unknown future felt so scary, I found enough clarity to make the very difficult decision to have a hysterectomy. I agonized over that decision and got three or four "second" opinions. The surgery ended up saving my life. My only regret is that I did not do it sooner. All of that burden of pain and worry over the future was largely gone within a couple of months because, as I discovered, the underlying sources of my pelvic pain were fibroids and endometriosis, which led to heavy, brutally painful periods. I applaud women who find a way to remediate their pelvic pain without surgery. However, in my case, a hysterectomy was absolutely necessary. After surgery I weaned myself off all medications and none are currently necessary! Yay!

Yoga helped me heal with ease after the surgery. My physical, mental, and emotional energy is so much stronger and more balanced now, and I only have occasional, mild pelvic pain and some bladder discomfort. Sometimes the pain flare-ups coincide with other inflammatory processes in my body. I have learned that my pelvic muscles tend to tense up with long periods of sitting, driving, or flying (which I offset with stretching sessions before and after), or extreme stress (such as death in the family). I am mostly pain free as long as I stick to my routine of exercise; water consumption; low acid, gluten-free, whole foods diet; and stress control.

There are times when despite my increased flexibility with my yoga practice, my body kind of locks up on itself, starting with the pelvic floor, but also my hips, knees, ankles, feet, shoulders, and back. It is much milder than it once was, but it still happens. It is unpredictable and I don't always know where this locking mechanism begins, but thanks to yoga I am more aware and better able to scan my body, detect issues, and address them. I have learned to control my breath so that it can help with thoughts, pain, and focus, and how to move the breath to and through the pelvis specifically to help the muscles relax and contract when they need to. I am constantly learning about my alignment, especially whether my tailbone is tucked under, which increases stress, and how to stretch my muscles and scan and compare sensation on one side versus the other. I feel good when friends comment on my improved posture. Yoga practice has increased the quality of my life. Leah speaks of the image of an elevator and a hammock, or thinking about the corners of the pelvic floor, its layers, and its movement. Imagery like this helps me understand. I don't love the marble/pebble image. Sorry, I don't like the idea of hard objects in my lady parts!

In my darker days, I read in online medical guidelines for pelvic pain that patients need emotional support and handholding, and that PT and yoga give them something to do and some control over their situation. I remember being offended when I read that I needed my hand held. But it was so true, especially at the beginning! A yoga instructor with specialized knowledge of the pelvic floor is a godsend. My health is a private thing, and I am not always forthcoming with details about my own issues, but I have found great benefit in sharing experiences and learning from others in a safe circle.

सत्य

Malasana– Deep Squat Pose

Stretches the Achilles tendons, hips, and pelvic floor, strengthens glutes and back

This deep squat can be challenging for many. You can modify it by placing a folded blanket under your heels, or by sitting on a block with the legs wide open, feet on the ground. **Do not do this pose if there is prolapse or a heavy feeling at the pelvic floor.**

Come to your deep squat with the toes pointing slightly out. Modify as needed. Ground your heels. The ankles, knees, and hips are soft, and your hands are in prayer position. Lengthen your spine and reach the crown of the head up; open your chest. Inhale and allow for the pelvic floor to relax (do not push, just release). Exhale, root your feet down and feel the energy rise in the opposite

direction collecting your pelvic floor in *isuf*. **Hold for several deep breaths.**

Squatting once was—and in many countries still is—a natural position for many everyday activities from elimination to washing laundry and preparing food. We can observe how toddlers naturally squat in this way when they learn to move in the world. As adults trying to relearn this position, we can feel very uncomfortable. The loss of ability to squat is a loss for the pelvic floor: when squatting, the pelvic floor is both stretched *and* exercised naturally. Throughout the day, and on the condition that you suffer no pain, play with this position, a couple of minutes here and there—don't worry about any patterns of breathing, don't overthink it, just hang out.

PRANAYAMA

"Observing the dusk and dawn of breathing, in which the pendulum changes its direction –the coolness of inhalation becomes the warmth of exhalation, drawing air into the body becomes a release outwards, the movement of air downward becomes the movement upward, the expansion of the ribcage becomes contraction, the inside becomes the outside, and vice versa–allows one to connect to the hidden in a direct and immediate way, untainted by the restricting influence of culture, language, religion, and faith. Every breath allows an unmediated experience of the unknown." *Priya Hart, In One Breath* [20]

प्राणायाम

We have spoken a lot about breathing. *Pranayama* is the Sanskrit for yogic breathing techniques directed at calming the nervous system, enhancing our lung capacity, balancing our energy level, and allowing for greater focus and concentration. *Prana* means life-energy, breath, respiration, spirit, vitality. *Ayama* means to lengthen, expand, restrain, control. *Pranayama* can be a bridge for our awareness to traverse into our deeper dimension, what is called in yoga *our true Self*–the divine within. Some of the classical breathing techniques that we practice in yoga are especially beneficial for pelvic floor health. These practices can assist with feeling the body more clearly and deeply, as well as with finding alignment. The next exercise–*kapalabhati*–is a wonderful addition to our practice because of its potential for training the muscles to collect rapidly when needed.

Emma (told by Leah)

Urine leakage ~ Scoliosis ~ Injuries ~ Hypertense muscles ~ Safe space

Emma shared with me how upset she was when she began buying protective pads, resigning herself to a new stage in her life. Small amounts of urine leakage after going to the bathroom had turned into "a large splotch." In her sixties, Emma is active and fashionable. She's always wearing a cute outfit with matching jewelry and nails, and I enjoy her spark. She confided that a part of her sadness regarding this condition was that she felt that she couldn't wear the clothes she desired any longer. She gave cute clingy dresses away, and moved her colorful leggings into storage from fear that they would reveal the pad too distinctly.

I met Emma in a pelvic health workshop. Emma later told me, "I was thrilled when I heard about your workshop. I wasn't convinced that it could truly help with my problem, but I was game to follow through." I remember very well my first impression of Emma. She was reserved, perhaps even slightly suspicious, and I was impressed with how well she protected her space. With significant scoliosis, and a variety of injuries in knees, shoulders, and neck from previous accidents and a result of her structure, she had learned how to be careful and attentive. Her hips too are unusually tight, inhibiting her range of movement and, as we discovered quite early, her pelvic floor muscles are overly contracted. She did not like my group class, and she wasn't shy about telling me in her well-appreciated direct manner. Her scoliosis, though she doesn't let it stop her doing anything she wants, does cause frustration if she cannot follow with the rest of the group.

Offering her the modifications she needed was challenging for me in that setting as well. I suggested private sessions, which she has been consistent with for several years now.

Emma's description of our private sessions as "totally nurturing and non-stressing" is important. How are we to ask our most intimate muscles to relax if we feel stressed or in a non-fostering environment? In addition to the external environment, her feeling of self-sovereignty is crucial for the success of our practice. Meanwhile, I convinced her to see a physical therapist specializing in pelvic health as well, and Emma was astonished when after several months of PT and yoga combined, her urinary leakage disappeared altogether. I reflect so fondly on her telling me that both the PT and I made it into her gratitude journal.

Emma loves the breathing exercise kapalabhati. She tells me over and over how special it feels to her, "It is helping me so much . . . calming and strengthening and meditative." The repetitive short exhalations we perform in kapalabhati and the holding of breath in between sequences, allows for the pelvic floor to both tone and release, the mind to stay focused, and the diaphragm to get a pleasant workout.

सत्य

Kapalabhati– Skull Shining Breath

Strengthens respiratory system, facilitates engaging and relaxing the core system, cleanses and warms

The slow breathing that you have practiced thus far has cultivated a bodily awareness and sometimes an enhancement of a certain pattern–the inhalation accompanied by a gentle downward movement and release of the pelvic floor, and the exhalation accompanied by a natural, gentle toning of the pelvic floor. We will now observe how the pelvic floor responds to the quicker, shorter breaths of *kapalabhati.* The ancient yoga text *Hatha Yoga Pradipika* describes this exercise as moving like the bellows of a blacksmith.[21] This description gives us a good idea of the amount of energy and heat that can be generated in this practice. Make sure you do not overdo it and get dizzy by going too fast. Slow down as much as needed.

- Sit up tall and cross-legged, or on a chair with your feet parallel on the ground. Root your feet and sitting bones. Inhale through the nostrils and allow your belly to relax. Make a series of 10–30 quick, rhythmic exhalations through your nose, with a passive inhalation rising in between (on each inhalation release your belly). Exhale all the air out. Take a slow expansive breath in and hold the breath for a long moment (as long as you are comfortable and feel no strain). Exhale and relax.
- Repeat this sequence once more, this time paying close attention to how your pelvic floor muscles respond to the breathing. Are the pelvic floor muscles still toning when you exhale and releasing a bit when you inhale?
- Now add a variation of *quick flicks*—what physical therapists often call quick contractive actions intended to train the pelvic floor muscles to contract spontaneously when inner abdominal pressure is created such as in sneezing. You want to be able to send a quick message to your pelvic floor to collect itself strongly when needed. Repeat *kapalabhati,* going slower for 10 breaths only. This time include a quick powerful *isuf* with every exhalation. Do not practice this if you experience any pain. Take a few slow, expansive breaths and relax your pelvic floor completely.

Lisa

Pelvic floor physical therapist ~ Caring for patients ~ Urine leakage ~ Birth injury ~ Prolapse ~ Alignment ~ Self-care

My pelvic floor journey began after the vaginal birth of my first child. I was 30 years old and had always been in good physical health. In the first weeks after delivery, I noticed urine leakage with coughing and sneezing, but it soon became apparent that I also leaked with walking and light jogging. I also noticed that my vagina felt different post-delivery. Upon inserting a finger, I felt something squishy at the opening where my once normal vagina used to reside. I remember thinking, "What the hell is this? Could this be what happens after having a baby and people don't talk about it?"

Due to a tear in the amniotic sac at forty weeks gestation, my labor was assisted with Pitocin. I labored for fourteen hours and pushed for two and a half. In the wee hours of the night, the midwife informed me that they would have to use the vacuum if I wasn't able to deliver soon. I had already had two episiotomies, yet I was getting nowhere. Fearing the vacuum, I bore down with all my might and felt a tearing sensation deep within me. I was sure the baby's head was out, but when I questioned this, both the midwife and my husband appeared confused. They both wondered why I would think the baby's head was out. What tore inside me? Approximately twenty minutes after this confusion, my son was born, changing my life forever. My focus shifted to my beautiful baby and the gratitude I felt to be a mother.

Less than one week postpartum, I began attending a local breastfeeding support group where I met other new moms. We became friends and often met up for outings. On an outing to a local state park, I worked up the courage to ask the other moms if they were experiencing any urinary leakage since having their first baby. I felt sure that they would confide that they too had this problem, and that we would commiserate. I was wrong. They all looked at me strangely and denied any such problem. Since this was 2003, online support was years from existing. I felt isolated. My OBGYN said everything looked great, but my vagina did not feel great, and I knew something was wrong.

Before my first baby, I worked as a physical therapist. It was a career I loved, and because of my education, I had a firm grasp on human anatomy and function. While studying the pelvic floor in college I discovered I couldn't stop the flow of urine when urinating, so I already thought that my pelvic floor muscles were weak. Now, as a new mom, with a new body, I felt lost. I felt as if I should be able to figure out how to help myself, and I was frustrated. I knew about pelvic floor muscles, and that I should be doing Kegels, but that is where my knowledge ended. I decided to be patient and allow my body to heal. I tried to do Kegels, but felt as if I couldn't adequately find the muscles. Over the next year my symptoms didn't worsen, but they also did not improve. Unfortunately, my physical therapy training in the 1990s offered very little in the area of pelvic health. Little did I know that I would learn there were more than a dozen pelvic floor muscles of which I had no knowledge. More surprisingly, I would come to understand that tightness in my pelvic floor muscles was the primary cause for my troubles.

Four years after the birth of my first child, I sought out a physical therapist who treated pelvic floor disorders. It seems crazy to think I waited that long, but life at home was very chaotic with three little ones so close in age. The therapist in my area was a woman who only assessed and treated the pelvic floor externally. While this was less than ideal, she did help me to somewhat "find" my pelvic floor with the aid of biofeedback and electrical stimulation. One year later, I joined the therapy team and began working alongside my therapist. In my search for more answers, I discovered coursework that would educate me in the internal assessment and treatment of pelvic floor disorders. It was in the first course that I learned I had a cystocele or bladder prolapse. I guess that explains the tearing sensation and the squishy feel at the entrance to my vagina. My doctor had examined me at least ten times since my first delivery and had never mentioned any abnormalities. I later learned that it is not uncommon for women to have some degree of prolapse after a vaginal delivery.

Much of my recovery can be attributed to a combination of body awareness, my physical therapy education, and intuition. My prolapse presented itself as heaviness in the vaginal area and sometimes it felt as if I had a bubble at the entrance to my vagina. My prolapse wasn't painful, but uncomfortable and annoying. Early on, in certain positions, my body would "take up" air through my vagina, only to release it with another position change. This was caused by excess bladder movement and was very embarrassing when it happened. I knew that prolapse could not be reversed, but only managed. Prolapse is not caused by muscle tearing, rather by damage to connective tissue like the endopelvic fascia. I learned to self-manage my prolapse by avoiding heavy lifting, straining, and repeated bouncing. I also learned that my bowels needed to stay regular and soft to avoid further prolapse symptoms. Much of my early recovery was wrought with anger and frustration. I wanted my vagina back! I wanted to be able to jump and run, but felt damaged. I was lucky to have a supportive husband who never made me feel as if things were different. I have been very successful in managing my prolapse and only occasionally feel symptomatic. I have come to terms with the fact that I cannot bounce on a trampoline, run, or do jump squats, and the like. My incentive for good prolapse management is not feeling my prolapse symptoms. I have reached a point where I rarely feel my prolapse and am able to enjoy walking, dancing, and yoga.

I discovered yoga approximately nine years after the birth of my son. It was the perfect balance of flexibility, stabilization, and mindfulness. My big breakthrough with Leah came when she identified my faulty posture. As I lengthened my body to adopt good posture, I was unknowingly lifting my ribcage up in front. As a therapist I know that the ribcage and the pelvis need to be "stacked" evenly to ensure correct core stability, but without the reinforcement I likely would have perpetuated this faulty posture. Leah has taught me patience with posture and also shown me the value of meditation.

Over the course of the last nine years, I have read countless articles, taken many continuing education classes, and connected the dots. I have learned that Kegels are not the magic cure-all they are touted to be, and that postnatal recovery is a journey. At work I now exclusively treat pelvic floor patients, and I know that my personal experience with pelvic floor dysfunction makes me a better physical therapist. My youngest patient has been five years old and the oldest in her nineties. They come to me with very personal problems and sometimes I am one of the few people they trust with their secret. I see women who have been unable to have intercourse with their partners due to pain and men who experience severe pain with ejaculation. I see both men and women who struggle with feeling like they have to pee all the time and those who cannot empty their bowels without severe pain. The list of various reasons people come to see me is quite long. The most important thing I have to offer my patients is education. If they can understand the mechanism behind their problem, then they will be more able to help themselves. I see improvements in patients who are willing to take an active role in their therapy. I know I'm in trouble when I see a patient who just wants me to "fix" them. Although everyone wants to be better quickly, most see gradual improvement over the course of three to nine months. The process is a journey.

I feel so lucky to share space with my patients and help them along their path to healing. It is my calling, formed by my own personal experience. I would be lying if I said I didn't think about what my life would be like if the doctors had taken me for an emergency C-section. I am very aware that the passion that I feel for my work would not be the same. I am also quite certain that I would still have pelvic floor problems, yet would not have the understanding to help myself. So yes, I am torn, quite literally and figuratively. For now, I will settle on the immense gratitude I feel for all the relationships I have forged as a result of this journey.

सत्य

Legs up the wall

Inverts the legs for relaxation and reversed blood flow, stretches hamstrings and back

I cannot stress enough how wonderful this posture is. Getting into it can be tricky! One of the ways to set up for this posture is to sit on the floor with the side of your hip close to the wall. Lie down on your side, roll onto your back, and bring your legs straight up the wall. Bring your sitting bones as close to the wall as possible; you may have some scooching forward or backward to do, but it is worth it! For certain conditions such as with pelvic pain, prolapse, or lower back pain, I recommend placing a folded blanket under your pelvis. Release your back and relax your shoulders, your sacrum is heavy. Observe the weight of your body and your head. Observe the touch of your heels on the wall. Rest your hands on your belly or lengthen them out to your side. Breathe deeply.

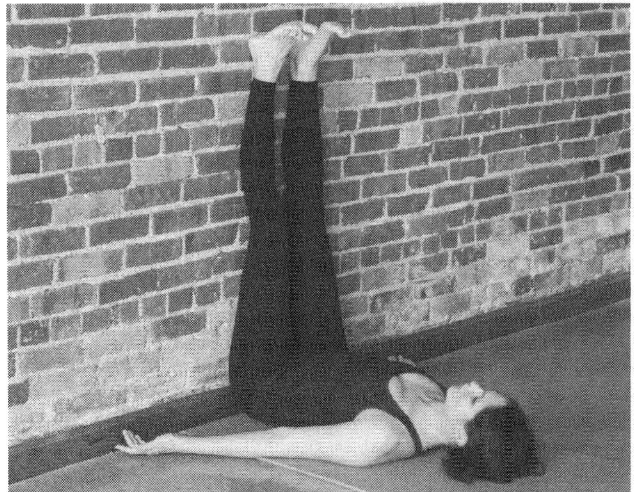

Hold this posture for 5–10 minutes.

अहिंसा

SPIRALING, FLOWING ENERGY OF BANDHAS

In Sanskrit, the word *bandha* means to *bind.* It refers to the action of binding energy in specific locations in the body–mainly the pelvic floor, diaphragm, and throat, but also to an extent in the feet and hands. By pressing upon blood vessels, nerves, and endocrine glands, bandhas control and influence circulation in the main organs and physiological systems of the body.[22] Traditionally, *bandhas* were taught in the context of *pranayama.* However, when practicing postures that require more strength, stability, and balance, as well as in dynamic transitions from *asana* to *asana,* experienced yoga practitioners can utilize their understanding of *bandhas* in a way that enhances and improves control of their movements.

Many moons ago, when I first immersed myself in yoga at a weekly Ashtanga yoga class in Jerusalem, the teacher explained that one should hold a particular *bandha–mula bandha,* or what is often translated as "root lock"–for the entire class. The instruction was to squeeze one's pelvic floor for an hour and a half straight–the only relief being in *savasana.* I remember feeling deeply uncomfortable on a physical level as a gripping sensation arose in my chest and throat, and on a mental level as it felt like a forceful, almost aggressive action, detached from what I thought yoga to be. I then felt guilty for being "not a good enough" student and for being unable to execute the teacher's instructions, as well as embarrassed for being so weak in my core. In retrospect, with what I have learned, I am grateful that I listened to my body and ignored this repeated instruction, as I now know that such a forceful localized clenching may have caused hypertense muscles and prevented me from experiencing two wonderful births. This is an example of how one-size-fits-all instruction can be harmful. It is also an example of how a poor understanding of *bandhas* can lead to a blocking of energy and organic movement, rather than the circulation of vital energy connecting the entire body.

When creating *bandhas,* we are not looking to simply trap energy in a region of the body. Dona Holleman and Orit Sen Gupta explain in *Dancing the Body of Light:*

> "Just "binding" the energy to a particular spot in the body would not make much sense. As in the cyclone, when the energy is compressed toward the center, the center is consequently pushed upward. . . . The art of distributing the energy throughout the body is to send it from *bandha* to *bandha,* thus connecting all the parts of the body."[23]

Uddiyana Bandha

We'll begin the practice of the bandhas with *uddiyana bandha*, which is commonly translated as "upward abdominal lock." *Uddiyana* means flying up. It can be performed in standing, forward fold, downward facing dog, lying down, or sitting. *Uddiyana bandha* provides a deeply comforting sensation of our internal space with a cleansing feeling of vitality and peace.

Practice *uddiyana bandha* on an empty stomach. In the table position, breathe in and let your belly relax. Then exhale completely. As you exhale, maintain the softness of the belly so that at the very end of the exhalation, without taking an inhale, you can suck the belly in and up, lifting the diaphragm gently upward. The ribcage lifts up as well. The feeling of suction, vacuum, and hollowing in the belly, and the level of release and relaxation needed to perform this *bandha* clarifies that the energy, while being held, is at once receptive and alive. Hold for a long, quiet moment, and then release the abdominal muscles slowly, allowing the belly to inflate again as you inhale gradually. As you practice let go of focusing on shape or alignment, but rather on sensation, allowing the pelvic floor and throat to respond.

MULA BANDHA

If you have practiced yoga before, you may have heard the term *mula bandha.* B.K.S. Iyengar, one of the greatest yoga authorities, describes *mula bandha* in his seminal book, *Light on Yoga*:

> "*Mula* means root, source, origin or cause, basis, or foundation. *Mula bandha* is the region between the anus and the scrotum. By contracting this region, *apana vayu* (the prana in the lower abdomen), whose course is downward, is made to flow up to unite with the *prana vayu*, which has its seat in the region of the chest."[24]

While it is clear from the text that Iyengar wrote as a man, for men, the area he refers to is the perineum, which can be a guideline for both men and women. Yet women may find additional space and power if they explore the front of their pelvic floor, mainly the vagina. Maximal activation is found if the pelvic floor feels balanced and active in all of its layers in unison.

While Iyengar describes the area of *mula bandha* in the body, he focuses on the upward energetic movement of *mula bandha.* So why are so many yoga teachers focused on localized squeezing? A student recently told me about a yoga class that ceremonially ends with "*mula bandha,*" with students instructed to raise their arms over head and then lower the hands into prayer position as they squeeze their bottoms. Is *mula bandha* simply about squeezing the glutes? Does the teacher want to say anus, but is too shy? And if she does just mean the anus, what about the other parts and layers of the pelvic floor?

I believe yoga teachers must use the term *mula bandha* with care, as the misconceptions and misunderstandings are many. Orit Sen-Gupta writes that through all her years of studying yoga with the great masters Iyengar, Pattabhi Jois, and Dona Holleman, *mula bandha* was never mentioned in the context of asana. She learned that bandhas are subtle, and that an excessive use of them can be harmful.[25] What are we trying to achieve then in *mula bandha*? And how does it connect to *isuf*? The power of *apana vayu* changing direction to rise upward, of which Iyengar speaks, is accessible when *isuf* is accessible. The ability to engage and control the pelvic floor muscles, and fine-tune where and what is moving *within* the pelvic floor in coordination with the belly drawing inwards, is what I believe we are looking for.

Mula bandha, then, can be thought of as an energetic form of *isuf*–both stronger and subtler, while being profoundly connected to the experience of *uddiyana bandha.* Just as *uddiyana bandha* is not about contracting and squeezing the abdominal muscles, *mula bandha* is far more than merely contracting and squeezing the pelvic floor. The vital, spiraling, bound energy of the *bandhas* lives best if the container–our body–is stable and grounded. Feeling the connection to the ground as you practice, and rooting your hands and feet with attention, greatly assists in finding this precise and powerful practice.

Mula Bandha in Sitting

Sit cross-legged or in a chair with your feet on the ground, the spine long. Inhale deeply. With the *beginning* of your exhalation spread your toes, gently rooting your feet down while creating a gentle *isuf.* Continue by drawing the navel back and lifting the diaphragm gently toward an *uddiyana bandha.* To accentuate and go deeper, hold the empty breath, allowing the chin to softly drop. Feel the flow of energy rising from the perineum to the navel, diaphragm, heart, and throat. Inhale deeply to release.

Remain attentive to your limits and sensitivity. In breathwork, as with postures, we do not want to agitate or exaggerate our movements in a way that will create new tensions or suffering.

अहिंसा

AN ORGANIC PART OF OUR WONDERFUL SELF

When I ask Katelyn at the end of our interview how she would summarize the ways yoga has benefited her, I am perplexed. She talks for some time about her body in general and how good she is feeling. She mentions a wonderful newfound awareness of breathing and a significant improvement in her mental health. *"And your pelvic floor . . . ?"* I ask leadingly. She pauses for a long moment. Then she kind of shrugs. And here, she teaches me what I have taught her: Her pelvic floor she says, well . . . is fine. It is just a part of her now.

There is one more concept in yoga that I would like to close with: *svadhyaya*–study of the self. *"To know thyself is the beginning of wisdom,"* says Socrates. We can learn about ourselves in many ways, and with attentive, thorough, and meaningful learning comes wisdom. The pelvic floor is just the pelvic floor. It is everything when things aren't going well, and it is just one part of our greater self when things are working as they should be. The work presented in this book is just one more way that we can learn more about who and how we are.

There is no magic to it, really, or perhaps it is all magical indeed. We repeat simple movements, breathe simple breaths. We are willing to be compassionate, truthful, and vulnerable with ourselves, and look at a place that might hold resistance, pain, or nothingness. Zooming in with our mind's eye, we study the base of the pelvis–the very center of our body–and see everything connecting to it and everything it is connected to. A healing path may reveal itself then. One that will allow us to feel whole, one in which the pelvic floor is simply an organic part of our wonderful self.

SAMPLE PRACTISE FLOWS

Here are some examples of short practices of about 15–20 minutes that you can follow. Feel free to blend them or create your own versions. The idea is for you find a way to have a daily practice that you enjoy and are committed to.

~ Relaxation
~ The diamond and its four corners
~ Gentle pelvic tilts
~ Bridge
~ Shhh on hands and knees
~ Downward facing dog

~ Happy baby
~ The pebble and the pearl
~ Squeezing and releasing a block
~ 90-degree angle
~ Bridge
~ Lotus opener

~ Legs up the wall

~ Skull-shining breath

~ Mountain

~ Chair

~ Deep squat

~ Thunderbolt

~ Leg stretches

~ The sphincters

~ Reclining bound angle: open and close

~ Hovering table

~ Locust

~ Cobra

~ *Uddiyana bandha* on hands and knees

~ Downwards facing dog

~ Deep squat

~ Chair

~ *Mula bandha*

~ Relaxation

ACKNOWLEDGMENTS

To Milie VandenBroek, I have my doubts if this book would have been written at all without your lasting, fierce, and loving support. You are the only person in the world I could have sent that first draft to, trusting in your honesty, sharpness of mind, and spot-on, poetic criticism. For your continuous encouragement, in doses I could take, and your belief in my voice, I thank you, my friend.

To Noga Barkai, meeting you changed the course of my life. A deep yearning for depth, and for certain qualities I could not yet name, sent me to countless yoga classes looking for *my* yoga teacher, perhaps not so unlike old myths describing wandering the forests in search of a guru. You have taught me yoga. You have taught me careful listening. You have taught me *ahimsa.*

To Orit Sen Gupta, for forming a language of yoga that I could instantly feel was home. For your rare ability to pour wisdom into each and every teaching. The first incarnation of this book was my final project, "The Pelvic Floor and Vijnana Yoga," for the teacher training with you. You challenged me with precise questions, you triggered something that crystalized my voice, you listened, and it is in large part your generous and trusting feedback that gave me the confidence and desire to transform my thesis into a book.

To Lisa Whiting, your professional support and openness from our very first conversation, your validation and readiness to collaborate, with your patients' best interest always in mind, is inspiring. Thank you for answering my strangest questions, being curious with me, and always having the time to discuss particularities. Thank you for your guidance. The world is a kinder place thanks to your sacred work.

To my editor Lisa Kremer, a huge thank you. Our encounter felt like it was meant to be and your ability to speak both the language of yoga and yet guide with wisdom through the world of words made me feel like my project was in the best possible hands. For all the extra caring you put in, I am thankful.

To my students who participated in the early days of my Integrated Pelvic Health classes, it will be challenging to articulate my thank you. For your reflective practice, willingness to experiment and be playful, and for sharing in detail what worked and what didn't, I am forever grateful. Your trust and your passion about the success of the class showed me just how important this safe space was. And how deeply needed more books on the topic are. To say I learned a lot from you would be an understatement. This book is the fruit of your practice.

And to the students who gave a piece of themselves in the form of their story to this book, thank you. I truly believe it will have an impact, and that you will be heard by someone who needs to hear just what you had to share.

To the beta readers, for your time, reflections, and advice, and for those who generously extended their expertise in translation, clarification, and editing. A special thanks to Adi Nachman, Elizabeth Short, Hadar Schwartz, Evan Fallenberg, Yoav Shamash,

Elizabeth Coggeshall, Cathy McClive, Lauriane Camus, Mark Stevens, and my sister Esther Wrobel.

For assisting with the photo shoot and making the experience fun, thank you Pat Gregory and Jodi Lawson. I can still taste that dirty chai we drank afterwards. Alicia Osborne, for your photography. Thank you for capturing the images with such authenticity. Another special thank you to Corinna Dodson. I am deeply moved every time I think about the hours you spent with me online, pushing me with your unique, loving stubbornness, to find more clarity in writing the practices. Dorit Talpaz, for your brilliance and sensitivity. My deepest gratitude for turning my words into a book.

To my mother Miriam, my two sisters Esther and Tovah, and to my terribly missed father Hal, thank you for continuously supporting me also through the difficult times and being proud no matter what. To my close friends, your belief in me and cheering on has meant the world. And to my husband, Doron Bauer, and our two magnificent children, Rohan and Orion, for your love.

ENDNOTES

[1] Fred M. Howard and others, eds., Pelvic Pain: Diagnosis and Management (Philadelphia: Lippincott Williams & Wilkins), 3–7.

[2] Leslie Howard, Pelvic Liberation: Using Yoga, Self-Inquiry and Breath Awareness for Pelvic Health, (California: Leslie Howard, 2017), 37.

[3] Eric Franklin, Pelvic Power: Mind/Body Exercises for Strength, Flexibility, Posture, and Balance for Men and Women, (New Jersey: Elysian Editions, 2003), 34.

[4] Amy Stein, Heal Pelvic Pain: The Proven Stretching, Strengthening, and Nutrition Program for Relieving Pain, Incontinence, I.B.S., and Other Symptoms Without Surgery, (New York: McGraw-Hill, 2008), 15.

[5] James L. Whiteside and Tyler Muffly, "Overview of Pelvic Floor Disorders: Epidemiology, Diagnosis, and Treatment," in Women and Health, ed. Marlene B. Goldman, Rebecca Troisi, Kathryn M. Rexrode, (London: Elsevier, 2013), 398–404.

[6] Amy Stein, Heal Pelvic Pain: The Proven Stretching, Strengthening, and Nutrition Program for Relieving Pain, Incontinence, I.B.S., and Other Symptoms Without Surgery, (New York: McGraw-Hill, 2008), 2.

[7] James L. Whiteside and Tyler Muffly, "Overview of Pelvic Floor Disorders: Epidemiology, Diagnosis, and Treatment," in Women and Health, ed. Marlene B. Goldman, Rebecca Troisi, Kathryn M. Rexrode, (London: Elsevier, 2013), 398–404.

[8] Amy Stein. Heal Pelvic Pain: The Proven Stretching, Strengthening, and Nutrition Program for Relieving Pain, Incontinence, I.B.S., and Other Symptoms Without Surgery, (New York: McGraw-Hill, 2008), 16.

[9] Katheryn Kassai and Kim Perelli, The Bathroom Key: Put an End to Incontinence, (New York: Demos Health, 2011), 23–30.

[10] Swami Satchidananda, The Yoga Sutras of Patanjali, (Integral Yoga Publications, 2012).

[11] Ina May Gaskin, Ina May's Guide to Childbirth, (New York: Bantam Books Trade Paperbacks, 2003), 182.

[12] These techniques draw directly from the seven vital principles of Vijnana yoga, the school of yoga that I have been practicing since 2003. Vijnana yoga's seven vital principles, outlined

by founder and master yoga teacher Orit Sen Gupta, are (1) relaxing the body, (2) awareness of breath, (3) quieting the mind, (4) focusing through intent, (5) rooting, (6) connecting, and (7) expanding. On my personal journey toward pelvic floor health, and in guiding others on their journey, I reexamined, shuffled, and reworded the Vijnana yoga vital principles to specially support the pelvic floor work that I wish to offer. Orit Sen Gupta, Vijnana Yoga Practice Manual, (Jerusalem: Vijnana Books, 2013).

[13] Leslie Kaminoff and Amy Matthews, Yoga Anatomy, (Champaign, 13 IL: Human Kinetics, 2011), 4–12.

[14] Michele Forsberg, "The Mysterious Connection Between Your Pelvis and Jaw," Align PT, 2018, https://www.alignpt.com/mysterious-connection-pelvis-jaw/.

[15] Ina May Gaskin, Ina May's Guide to Childbirth, (New York: Bantam Books Trade Paperbacks, 2003), 170.

[16] Katy Bowman, Alignment Matters, (Propriometrics Press, 2016), 157.

[17] Ibid, 18.

[18] Stéphanie J. Madill and Linda McLean, "Relationship Between Abdominal and Pelvic Floor Muscle Activation and Intravaginal Pressure During Pelvic Floor Muscle Contractions in Healthy Continent Women," Neurourology and Urodynamics, 25, no. 7 (2006), https://doi.org/10.1002/nau.20285.

[19] Blandine Calais-Germain, Anatomy of Movement, (Seattle: Eastland Press, 1993), 235.

[20] Priya Hart, B'Neshima Echat [In One Breath], (Israel: Modan, 2012), 45. (Quotation translated from the Hebrew by Leah Wrobel.)

[21] Swami Muktibodhananda, Hatha Yoga Pradipika. (Munger, Bihar, India: Yoga Publications Trust, 2001), 220.

[22] Orit Sen Gupta, Vayu's Gate: Yoga and the Ten Vital Winds, (Jerusalem: Vijnana Books, 2014), 33.

[23] Dona Holleman and Orit Sen Gupta, Dancing the Body of Light: The Future of Yoga, (Netherlands: Pandion Enterprises, 2000), 38–39.

[24] B.K.S Iyengar, Light on Yoga, (New Delhi: Harper Collins Publishers, 2001), 437.

[25] Orit Sen Gupta, Vayu's Gate: Yoga and the Ten Vital Winds, (Jerusalem: Vijnana Books, 2014), 34.

BIBLIOGRAPHY

Arzi-Padan, Mira. *Yoga Nashit [Yoga for Women].* Israel: *Kol haguf hafakot,* 2014.

Burch, Vidyamala and Penman, Danny. *Mindfulness for Health (Enhanced Edition): A Practical Guide to Relieving Pain, Reducing Stress and Restoring Wellbeing.* London: Piatkus, 2013.

Calais-Germain, Blandine. *The Female Pelvis: Anatomy and Exercises.* Seattle: Eastland Press, 2003.

Cohan, Wendy. *The Better Bladder Book: A Holistic Approach to Healing Interstitial Cystitis and Chronic Pelvic Pain.* New York: Hunter House, 2011.

Franklin, Eric. *Pelvic Power: Mind/Body Exercises for Strength, Flexibility, Posture, and Balance for Men and Women.* New Jersey: Elysian Editions, 2003.

Gaskin, Ina May. *Ina May's Guide to Childbirth.* New York: Bantam Books Trade Paperbacks, 2003.

Gaskin, Ina May. *Spiritual Midwifery.* Summertown, TN: Book Publishing Company, 2002.

Hart, Priya. *B'Neshima Echat* [In One Breath]. Israel: Modan, 2012.

Hodges, P.W., Sapsford, R., and Pengel, L.H.M., "Postural and Respiratory Functions of the Pelvic Floor Muscles." *Neurology and Urodynamics* 26, no. 3 (2007), https://doi.org/10.1002/nau.20232.

Holleman, Dona and Sen-Gupta, Orit. *Dancing the Body of Light: The Future of Yoga.* Netherlands: Pandion Enterprises, 2000.

Howard, Leslie. *Pelvic Liberation: Using Yoga, Self-Inquiry and Breath Awareness for Pelvic Health.* California: Leslie Howard, 2017.

Iyengar, B.K.S. *Light on Yoga.* New Delhi: Harper Collins Publishers, 2001.

Kaminoff, Leslie and Matthews, Amy. *Yoga Anatomy.* Champaign, IL: Human Kinetics, 2011.

Kassai, Katheryn and Perelli, Kim. *The Bathroom Key: Put an End to Incontinence.* New York: Demos Health, 2011.

Kitani, Lenore, PT. "Pelvic Floor Activity and Breathing in Women." Trial. Texas Tech University Health Sciences Center, (2012), https://clinicaltrials.gov/ct2/show/NCT01694979.

McInnes, Kerry. *Modern Yoga: Everything You Want to Know About the Pelvic Floor.* E-Book: Shut Up and Yoga Library, 2019.

Muktibodhananda Saraswati, Swami. *Hatha Yoga Pradipika.* Bihar, India: Yoga Publications Trust, 1993.

Nagoski, Emily. *Come as You Are (the Surprising New Science that Will Transform Your Sex Life).* Simon & Schuster, 2015.

Satchidananda, Swami. *The Yoga Sutras of Patanjali.* Yogaville, Virginia: Integral Yoga Publications, 2011.

Sen-Gupta, Orit. *The Heart of Practice: Understanding Yoga from Inside.* Vijnana Books, 2014.

Sen-Gupta, Orit. *Vayu's Gate: Yoga and the Ten Vital Winds.* Vijnana Books, 2014.

Stein, Amy. *Heal Pelvic Pain: The Proven Stretching, Strengthening, and Nutrition Program for Relieving Pain, Incontinence, IBS, and Other Symptoms Without Surgery.* New York: McGraw-Hill, 2008.

Made in the USA
Las Vegas, NV
28 April 2023

71251135R00098